Friends of God

American University Studies

Series VII
Theology and Religion

Vol. 76

PETER LANG
New York · San Francisco · Bern
Frankfurt am Main · Paris · London

Paul J. Wadell, C.P.

Friends of God

Virtues and Gifts in Aquinas

PETER LANG
New York · San Francisco · Bern
Frankfurt am Main · Paris · London

BV
4817
.W33
1991

Library of Congress Cataloging-in-Publication Data

Wadell, Paul J.
　　Friends of God : virtues and gifts in Aquinas /Paul J.
Wadell.
　　　　p. cm. — (American university studies. Series VII,
Theology and religion ; vol. 76)
　　Includes bibliographical references.
　　1. God—Worship and love—History of doctrines—
Middle Ages, 600-1500.　2. Charity—History of
doctrines—Middle Ages, 600-1500.　3. Theological
virtues—History of doctrines—Middle Ages,
600-1500.　4. Gifts, Spiritual—History of doctrines—
Middle Ages, 600-1500.　5. Thomas, Aquinas, Saint,
1225?-1274.　　I. Title.　II. Series: American university
studies. Series VII, Theology and religion ; v. 76.
BV4817.W33　　1991　　241'.4'092—dc20　　91-10919
ISBN 0-8204-1321-6　　　　　　　　　　　　　CIP
ISSN 0740-0446

CIP-Titelaufnahme der Deutschen Bibliothek

Wadell, Paul J.:
Friends of God : virtues and gifts in Aquinas / Paul J.
Wadell.—New York; Berlin; Bern; Frankfurt am Main;
Paris: Lang, 1991
　(American university studies : Ser. 7, Theology and
religion ; Vol. 76)
　ISBN 0-8204-1321-6
NE: American university studies / 07

© Peter Lang Publishing, Inc., New York 1991

Printed in the United States of America.

Table of Contents

Introduction

The idea for this book formed slowly. In the Fall of 1981 I took a course in Aristotle and Kant with Professor Stanley Hauerwas, then of the University of Notre Dame. When reading the *Nichomachean Ethics*, I was taken with Aristotle's splendid discussion of friendship, and especially intrigued that at the end of his reflections on friendship he writes, "So let us begin our discussion." Was this an invitation to re-read the *Nichomachean Ethics* and envision the moral life from the perspective of friendship?

A few months later I began to read Thomas Aquinas's brilliant account of the moral life in his *Summa Theologiae*, making my way through his study of human action, happiness, the passions and emotions, the virtues, and the Gifts of the Spirit. It was dazzling, but also overwhelming. Was there a key to its intricacy? I thought there might be in Aquinas's definition of charity as friendship with God. It seemed to me that Thomas was using this understanding of charity to extend Aristotle's invitation to consider the moral life as a life of friendship; but more than that, I wondered if charity functioned for Aquinas as the cornerstone of his moral theology. Could it be considered as the interpretative key to the *Prima Secundae*? If so, would it reveal an interconnectedness between his account of the passions, the virtues, and the Gifts of the Spirit that otherwise might be missed? The project of this book is to answer that question.

Accordingly, chapter one examines what Aquinas means in speaking of charity as a friendship we have with God, and why this friendship is not only a single virtue, but the constitutive activity of the Christian moral life. Aquinas's understanding of friendship and its importance in the moral life is substantiated in light of Aristotle's more detailed explication in the *Nichomachean Ethics*. Aquinas accepted Aristotle's description of friendship and its importance as a setting for learning and developing the virtues, but went beyond Aristotle in proposing that our primary moral relationship must be a friendship with God. This first chapter concludes with a discussion of why this sharing in the life of God is our happiness, and why such happiness pivots on acquiring a likeness to God so complete that we are able to consider God another self.

Chapter two begins with an analysis of Aquinas's account of the passions from the perspective of charity-friendship with God. What becomes clear from this study is the primacy of love in the Thomistic moral schema. For Aquinas, the successful outcome of the moral life depends on learning to love the right things in the right way; we must love most what will make us both happy and good. This is why charity must be the sovereign love of all those who find happiness in God. As we shall see, Aquinas calls us to be God's friends not only because God deserves our love, but also because if what we love has such inescapable impact on who we become and the happiness possible to us, then our greatest passion has to be for God. Finally, what will be most striking in this study of the passion of love is the very different understanding it gives us of the virtues. Once we see the connection Aquinas makes between the passions and the virtues, we will also discover that although there may be similarities between his account of the virtues and Aristotle's, there are also some startling differences.

In chapter three we begin a discussion of the virtues. Aquinas has an ethic of virtue because he saw the virtues as characteristic ways of acting capable of achieving the transformation we must undergo in order to become good. We are called to become more than we already are; in fact, we are called to undergo a transfiguration so complete that God can come to look at us not as sinner, but as friend. This conversion to godliness is the harvest of virtues born from charity's love. This chapter will examine Aquinas's understanding of the virtues, but always underscoring the special and inseverable connection he sees between all the virtues and charity. In Aquinas's account of the moral life, there could be no true virtue that was not formed from charity-friendship with God. The chapter concludes by considering what Aquinas means in calling charity the "form" of the virtues, and how he sees charity redefining our estimation of a virtue's standard of goodness.

Most studies of Thomistic ethics overlook Aquinas's treatise on the Gifts of the Spirit; however, once it is grasped that the virtues emerge from the passions and are at the service of charity, the Gifts become central. The final chapter will study how Aquinas understood the Gifts of the Spirit, how he saw them functioning, and why for him they represented not an appendage to his account of the Christian moral life, but the perfection of charity's virtues. The Gifts of the Spirit are in no way an afterthought to Aquinas's account of the virtues, but the fullness of virtues designed to make us friends with God. Put differently, for Aquinas the Gifts of the Spirit are not superfluous to the virtues, but exactly the kinds of activities for which charity's virtues prepare. The Gifts are the perfection of friendship with God because we are most fully an "other self" to God when God is the principle of all we do. When God's Spirit is fully alive in us we know love, peace, and joy. Thomas calls these the Fruits of the Spirit, and it is in possessing them that the moral life is completed.

This book grew out of a dissertation project at the University of Notre Dame. There are several people to thank. A special debt of gratitude belongs to Professor Stanley Hauerwas, now of Duke University, who directed this project and guided me through three years at Notre Dame. He is a fine man, a tremendous teacher, and a good friend. A mark of how much I learned from Professor Hauerwas is seen in how differently I think about ethics now than I did before I met him. Anyone even remotely familiar with his writings will see his influence throughout this book. A word of thanks is also due Professors David Burrell, Robert Wilken, and John Howard Yoder. That they were able to see so much that I missed and recognize problems where I saw none, made for a significantly revised and hopefully better book. I am grateful not only for their criticisms and suggestions, but also for the support and encouragement they offered.

I would not have had this opportunity to study the ethics of Aquinas if it had not been offered me by my Passionist Community.

I am grateful to them for granting me the time to pursue this project, and especially thankful for the encouragement and support I have received from my Passionist brothers here at Catholic Theological Union in Chicago. Special thanks must be extended to Sebastian MacDonald, C.P. Before he became our Provincial, Rev. MacDonald was a professor of ethics at Catholic Theological Union. He was my first mentor in the field of ethics and remains a trusted guide, teacher, and friend.

At the beginning of my research on the book, I traveled to Toronto to examine the resources of the Pontifical Institute of Medieval Studies at St. Michael's University. I am grateful to Donald Finlay, C.S.B., librarian of the Institute, for so generously making the library available to me, and Professors Osmund Lewry, O.P., James Weisheipl, O.P., and Walter Principe, C.S.B., for the hospitality they offered and the assistance they gave at the early stages of my research.

Finally, I must thank my family, especially my parents, for the untiring concern they showed me while this was being done. I know my interest in this topic of friendship with God was sparked by the love I have always witnessed and received from them. They were the ones who taught me first and best that being friends of God enables us to know what it means to be good friends with anyone else.

To the Memory

of

James Patrick White, C.P.

and

Steven Mudd, C.P.

Chapter I

Charity as Friendship with God

The purpose of this book is simple. I want to show how focusing on Aquinas's definition of charity as friendship with God offers a better understanding of his treatises on the passions, the virtues, and the Gifts of the Spirit. Aquinas's moral theology, set forth in his *Summa Theologiae*, particularly in the *Prima Secundae*, has been read in many ways, but the argument of this book is that if it is read under the rubric of charity, where charity as friendship with God becomes an interpretative key for understanding the *Prima Secundae*, then not only will Aquinas's account of the passions, the virtues, and the Gifts be read differently, but there will also appear a cohesiveness among these parts of the *Prima Secundae* that otherwise might be missed.

Thomas's account of the virtues has been amply and richly examined, and its uniqueness underscored; but it has not been shown that precisely how Thomas understands the virtues, particularly in their connection to the passions and the Gifts, can be read as a function of charity-friendship with God. Consequently, what we shall suggest is that if one understands what Thomas means by charity as friendship with God and how that functions as something of a metaphor for the Christian moral life, then not only will his account of the virtues be better appreciated, but it will also be clear why what he says about the virtues cannot be separated from what he says about the passions and the Gifts. True, what Thomas means by calling charity friendship with God has been considered by many commentators, most recently Tibor Horvath and Albert Ilien,[1] but it is customarily examined independently of the account of the Christian moral life he presents in the *Prima Secundae*. Correspondingly, how a reading of the *Prima Secundae* might be illumined from the perspective of charity as friendship with God has not been attempted.

Thus, we will examine Thomas's treatment of the passions, the virtues, and the Gifts of the Spirit through the constitutive virtue of the Christian life, charity-friendship with God, and argue that if charity is used as a principle of interpretation for the *Prima Secundae*, the genius of Thomas's moral theology will be more fully disclosed. To begin then we shall consider first what Thomas meant in calling charity a friendship we have with God, and why he insisted that friendship is our happiness.

A. What it Means to Call Charity Friendship with God

For Thomas, charity is friendship with God. And when he writes in the *Prima Secundae* that "charity signifies not only the love of God, but also a certain friendship with him,"[2] he has in mind a very special, distinct relationship with God that must be characterized by certain qualities determinative of friendship. By identifying charity as friendship, Thomas is claiming that not any relationship of the Christian with God is acceptable, but only a relationship of friendship. Friendship properly names what is to exist between God and ourselves. What joins us to God is the bond of friendship, and, as Thomas insists, this means not only that God loves us, but also that we love God, and that our love for God be formed according to the very particular rigors of friendship. By defining charity as friendship, Aquinas suggests not only that charity signals a relationship of a special kind, but also that we do not rightly love God unless our love is marked by the criteria proper to friendship. As Edouard Gagnon suggests, if "la charité...est une vertu dans la mesure même où elle est une amitié,"[3] that also means we can only truly love God when we have learned what it means to be God's friend.

It is in question twenty-three of the *Secunda Secundae* that Thomas gives a more detailed look at what it means to call charity friendship with God. In this passage, following Aristotle, Aquinas remarks that "not all love has the character of friendship,"[4] but only that love which exhibits three special qualities. We will consider them briefly here. First, friends are recognized as those who wish well to each other, those who "so love another as to will what is good for him." This first mark of friendship is simply our desire to wish what is good for our friend because it is good for our friend, and to wish it for the sake of our friend. Secondly, genuine friendship is characterized by reciprocity. There is and can be no friendship where the good will we have toward others is not also wished for us by them. As Thomas says, "Good will alone is not enough for friendship for this requires a mutual loving; it is only with a friend that a friend is friendly." This qualification is important not just because of the obvious fact that there can be no friendship where the one who loves as a friend is not also loved in kind, but also because to make reciprocity a distinguishing mark of friendship indicates that as a friendship it is a life activity eventually scored by a certain likeness or equality of love. This means, as we shall examine in greater detail later, that part of Aquinas's strategy in naming charity friendship is to propose that the always unfinished task of the Christian life, a task that indeed becomes our beatitude, is to endeavor to love as God loves us. Consequently, to make reciprocity a requirement of friendship signifies that through the very activity of friendship, each friend eventually becomes a reflection of the other because each is like the other in what he or she considers good.

It is this shared good, a good which bonds them together in friendship, that is the third and most important element of friendship. Each of the qualities Thomas highlights as necessary for friendship can count toward the making of friendship only insofar as they are connected to the succeeding one. For example, Thomas says desiring what is good for another is the first sign of friendship, but such is a friendship only insofar as what the one wishes for the other is also wished by the other for him. Benevolence makes a relationship a friendship in the measure that it is mutual; however, Thomas adds, reciprocity does not precede, but is a sign that something is shared in common. The good that friends share is the singlemost important element of friendship because the quality of that good determines the quality of the friendship. When Thomas says every friendship is based on what friends share in common, he implies that what makes the friendship, and thereby determines the character of the friends, is the genuineness of this good. To this extent, friendship is immediately a function not so much of any quality intrinsic to the friends, but of the good that is loved by both and which, in turn, makes both the friends and their friendship good.

This is an important point for correctly approaching how the moral life is to be understood as a life of friendship because it means the quality and depth of any friendship, its perfection and therefore its intimacy, depends entirely on the kind of good friends share. Friendship is known by benevolence and mutuality strictly because it is the activity of delighting with another in the same good, and wishing for the other the very good she wishes for us, not only because we each desire this good, but also because friendship occurs only insofar as we each possess it. For example, intimacy in friendship is not the result of directly seeking it; rather, intimacy comes from desiring a good that is loved by both of us. To this extent, we enter the life of another not by a love that overcomes them, but by a love that appreciates and shares what he or she most considers good.

Applied to charity, Thomas says the shared good that forms the basis of our friendship with God is the very happiness of God. "Now there is a sharing of man with God," Thomas explains, "by his sharing his happiness with us, and it is on this that friendship is based." The relationship we have with God is and can be a friendship not only because God shares with us a good from which a friendship can begin, but also more decisively because the good God communicates to us-this good of God's very happiness-is exactly the good the full possession of which makes possible the appropriate perfection of our lives. All this will be examined further as the chapter unfolds, but for now what is crucial is to see that the kind of good God shares with us in establishing the friendship of charity makes absolutely all the difference. It is only this particular good that establishes a friendship that enables us to be formed in the character of God.

Accordingly, in the Thomistic rendering of charity as friendship, everything pivots on how the good God shares with us is understood. The good we wish for God and that God desires for us, the reciprocity which exists between us, and even the eventual identification of ourselves as God's friends, is contingent upon the good from which our friendship emerges and which establishes its constitutive activity. It is the good God shares with us that tells us what our friendship with God can be, what is its most fitting expression as well as its ultimate goal. To this extent, it is not quite right to say as Pinckaers does that the gift of self shown in the reciprocity of friendship is "la source et la loi de l'amitié;"[5] rather, as DeBroglie suggests, the source of friendship is participation in a shared good.[6]

All this is but a brief summary of what Thomas means by friendship and what precisely is the good by which charity is constituted. We shall examine this more fully as the chapter unfolds. For now, however, to appreciate more adequately what Thomas means by friendship we must turn to Aristotle, for when Thomas structures his account of friendship he works from an understanding of this relationship outlined more precisely by this philosopher.

B. Aristotle's Influence on the Thomistic Account of Friendship

Aristotle begins his discussion of friendship in Book VIII of *The Nichomachean Ethics*, and while not quite sure how friendship is related to morality, claims that "it is some sort of excellence or virtue, or involves virtue, and it is, moreover, most indispensable for life" because "no one would choose to live without friends, even if he had all other goods."[7] At this point, Aristotle is working to uncover the precise significance of friendship for his ethics. He had spoken earlier of happiness, the virtues, and the proper function of men and women; and now, without any intimation, but with simply the assertion that "continuing in a sequence, the next subject which we shall have to discuss is friendship," begins to plot the place of friendship in the moral life. At this point in his lectures, Aristotle realizes that through friendships with good people we "get some sort of training in virtue or excellence,"[8] but it is not until the closing line of *The Nichomachean Ethics* when Aristotle says, "Now let us begin," that the reader suspects Aristotle, having grown skeptical that a polity of men and women in a common good would ever be a reality, turns to friendship as a more promising center for the moral life. However implicitly, it is now the polity of friendship, the life shared between those joined in their love for the good, that best represents what the moral life is to be. The clue dangling at the end of *The Nichomachean Ethics* suggests not only that friendship is important for morality, but more pointedly, that the moral life is friendship because it is what happens in friendships between men and women who are good that not only teaches them what it means to be good, but also endows them with the virtues through which they become good.

In his excellent article, "Aristotle on Friendship," John M. Cooper notes that according to Aristotle, friendship, "taken most generally, is any relationship characterized by mutual liking as this is defined in the *Rhetoric*, that is, by mutual well-wishing and well-doing out of concern for one another."[9]　Furthermore, Cooper adds, "A friend wishes well to his friend for his friend's own sake."[10] Cooper convincingly argues[11] that this general description of friendship applies to the three kinds of friendship specified by Aristotle: friendships based on usefulness, friendships based on pleasure, and friendships based on goodness or virtue.[12] Each of these friendships is distinguished according to what forms the bond between friends, a point which confirms our earlier insight that what identifies and forms a friendship is the good shared between the friends.[13]

Nonetheless, although friendships of usefulness and friendships of pleasure fit the general description of friendship, for Aristotle "these two kinds are friendships only incidentally, since the object of affection is not loved for being the kind of person he is, but for providing some good or pleasure."[14] That which is friendship truly is friendship based on goodness or virtue:

The perfect form of friendship is that between good men who are alike in excellence or virtue. For these friends wish alike for one another's good because they are good men, and they are good per se, (that is, their goodness is something intrinsic, not incidental). Those who wish for their friends' good for their friends' sake are friends in the truest sense, since their attitude is determined by what their friends are and not by incidental considerations. Hence their friendship lasts as long as they are good, and that means it will last for a long time, since goodness or virtue is a thing that lasts.[15]

Cooper prefers to call this "central and basic kind of friendship...friendship of character" instead of a "virtue friendship" or "friendship of the good," because "the expression 'character-friendship' brings out accurately that the basis for the relationship is the recognition of good qualities of character, without in any way implying that the parties are moral heroes."[16] He explains:

Such friendships exist when two persons, having spent enough time together to know one another's character and to trust one another (1156b25-29), come to love one another because of their good human qualities....Each, loving the other for his good qualities of character, wishes for him whatever is good, for his own sake, precisely in recognition of his goodness of character, and it is mutually known to them that well-wishing of this kind is reciprocated (1156a3-5).[17]

Still, perhaps what most commands our attention is not Aristotle's general point that "it is...in the friendship of good men that feelings of affection and friendship exist in their highest and best form,"[18] but that in his analysis Aristotle establishes a relationship between the kind of good mutually adhered to that makes friendship possible, and the similarity in goodness between friends that is friendship's work to achieve. Friendship is the dynamic, vital activity whereby those devoted to what is good are, in the crucible of friendship, gradually chiseled into people alike in goodness. Cooper is right to say, "Hence a human being cannot have a flourishing life except by having intimate friends to whom he is attached precisely on account of their good qualities of character and who are similarly attached to him: it is only with such persons that he can share the moral activities that are most central to his life."[19]

That is exactly Aristotle's point. One cannot have a fully human life without friends because it is only in friendship that the sharing of the kinds of activities constitutive of a good life can be sustained. It is not just that friendship makes morally good activity more interesting and pleasant, but that indeed it makes it possible, for friendship is the locus of the kinds of virtuous activities whereby one who delights in the good actually becomes good. In short, the moral value of friendship for Aristotle is that this similarity in goodness that represents the perfection of friendship,[20] can never occur outside the context of friendship because it is exactly friendship, as the ongoing, mutual, delighting in the good, that makes such perfection of character possible.

Aristotle uncovers a process in friendship that parallels what Aquinas takes to happen in the friendship with God he calls charity. As we shall see, what Aquinas gleans from Aristotle is the insight that while friendship may describe a relation between those who recognize in each other a love for the same good, friendship, morally speaking, must always be understood not passively, but as the delightful activity of mutually pursuing and nurturing in one another the good that bonds them in friendship and finally makes them one. In this sense, through the life of friendship the similarity crucial to friendships of virtue deepens. Initially, friends are similar because they desire the same good; however, it is this desire embodied in activity and woven through the life of the friendship that eventually accounts for a similarity in goodness that is no longer extrinsic, but is instead characteristic of the friends. Friendship is the locus of moral development, the place where moral transformation occurs, because it is in friendship that the project of the moral life to become the very thing we love takes place.

And so when Aristotle talks about the perfection of friendship,[21] we know it is achieved only when the friends have been determined or characterized by a shared good. The goal of friendship, which is also friendship's great possibility, is a similarity in goodness or virtue the very likeness of which enables each to see the other as his or her self; however, that happens only through the exchange of friendship whereby both, in their desire for the other's well-being, are formed by and into whatever they love. While all this now may seem only remotely connected to Thomas's account of charity as friendship, it later becomes crucial when we consider that for Thomas the principle work of charity is to form us into the likeness of a God who as our friend is also our good.

Secondly, in order to appreciate further how Aristotle provides the tradition from which so much of Aquinas's treatise on charity as friendship can be illumined, especially the relationship Aquinas forges between charity and beatitude, it is necessary to consider the link Aristotle stitches between happiness and virtue. It is clear from the opening paragraphs of *The Nichomachean Ethics* that Aristotle is fashioning an eudemonistic ethic, but we miss the force of this claim unless we remember that for Aristotle happiness or "eudaimonia" is the virtuous life. To identify happiness, Aristotle looks to human experience and concludes that happiness is that "for the sake of which everything else is done," that "which is pursued as an end in itself" and not "for the sake of something else....We see then," Aristotle writes, "that happiness is something final and self-sufficient and the end of our actions."[22] Aristotle isolates happiness as the driving force of life, that which empowers and motivates all that we do for in everything, beyond the specific end of any particular action, we necessarily seek happiness as the consummate good of life.

Nevertheless, it would be a mistake to read Aristotle and conclude that he views happiness as but the result of virtue, an end product to which virtue is simply the means; on the contrary, Aristotle insists that happiness is not the residue of activity, but is, rather, itself "some sort of activity," and the activity alone which is "desirable in itself and not for the sake of something else." What would such an activity be? "Activities desirable in themselves," Aristotle responds, "are those from which we seek to derive nothing beyond the actual exercise of the activity. Actions in conformity with virtue evidently constitute such activities; for to perform noble and good deeds is something desirable for its own sake."[23] Far from separating the virtues and happiness, Aristotle fuses them so that there exists a tight internal correspondence between eudaimonia and the virtuous life. Eudaimonia, far from being something distinct from virtue or even the prize of virtue,

and far from being something for which the virtues are purely a
preparatory exercise, is itself the virtuous life. In identifying
happiness with the virtues and insisting that happiness is not
separate from the virtues but descriptive of the virtuous life,
Aristotle so tightly bonds goodness with happiness and the virtues
with human flourishing that it becomes impossible to think any
longer of happiness as that which represents the possession of
whatever we choose to desire, but demands that we consider
happiness as that which comes from learning both to desire and to
achieve the goodness that is most appropriately ours. Again, as we
shall soon detail, Aristotle's argument renders more coherent
Thomas's own insistence that happiness is not something which
stands apart from or is a consequence of charity, but is instead the
life of friendship with God straining toward a perfection Thomas
calls beatitude.

Still, to insist that happiness is the virtuous life is to make an in-
exact, vague, and even uninteresting claim unless it is clear there is
some point in being virtuous. To assert that eudaimonia and the
virtuous life are one begs the question of why being virtuous counts
for happiness. Aristotle cannot possibly sustain the identity he
forges between happiness and the virtuous life unless he likewise
identifies the end or goal which makes the very activity of the
virtues intelligible, and which seals the connection between eudaimonia and the virtues by suggesting that our very participation in
the end is possible only through the activity of the virtues that me-
diate the end. In order to make sense of his connection between
happiness and the virtues, Aristotle has to pinpoint that for which
the virtues exist, because the virtues are not intelligible in themselves, but only in the end they serve.

Aristotle answers this challenge by saying there is something all
men and women are to become, a goal or telos that represents the
fitting perfection of our lives; but again, this telos is not so much
something that stands apart from us as the culmination of human
behavior, but is instead the activity of what Aristotle calls our
"proper function." Implicit in Aristotle's conclusion is his contention that there is for all of us some singlemost function the ac-

tivity of which best represents what it means to be human. Happiness and virtue coincide only when virtue flows from and expresses that activity or function, the performance of which correspondingly achieves the telos or goal of our nature. As Aristotle explains, "To call happiness the highest good is perhaps a little trite" and needs to be supplemented by "first ascertaining the proper function of man. For just as the goodness and performance of a flute player, a sculptor, or any kind of expert, and generally of anyone who fulfills some function or performs some action, are thought to reside in his proper function, so the goodness and performance of man would seem to reside in whatever is his proper function." It is incredible to Aristotle that men and women would "be left by nature a good-for-nothing without a function," so he must assume that "just as the eye, the hand, the foot, and in general each part of the body clearly has its own proper function, so man too has some function over and above the function of his parts," even though at the end of this passage he intriguingly asks, "What can this function possibly be?"[24]

Aristotle does not answer this question until the tenth and final book of *The Nichomachean Ethics*, but even so, at this point he at least enables us to see that there is some one thing that men and women can do that is not only the activity which is most distinctively and characteristically theirs, but is also that activity by which their telos is incipiently enjoyed. Consequently, Aristotle focuses the connection between happiness and virtue by teaching that if "the good of man is an activity of the soul in conformity with excellence or virtue, and if there are several virtues," human happiness is the activity "in conformity with the best and most complete."[25] In other words, for Aristotle happiness is a sharing in whatever activity best enables the fullness of our natures. As he puts it, happiness "is at once the best, noblest, and most pleasant thing" precisely because it describes that through which our perfection is achieved.[26]

What is that activity? Aristotle reasons that the most perfect human happiness would be an activity that is not only in conformity with virtue, but also one that conforms to the highest virtue, the "virtue of the best part of us," which corresponds to "the most divine thing in us." It is "the activity of this part," he concludes, "when operating in conformity with the excellence or virtue proper to it that will be complete happiness."[27] Put differently, happiness for women and men is to participate in whatever activity conforms to their noblest possibility.

But notice Aristotle's strategy. By identifying happiness as an activity which conforms "to the most divine thing in us," he suggests that we are happy insofar as we become as like as possible to the very beings we are not, the gods. The proper function of men and women, indeed their telos, is to engage themselves in that activity which allows them to come closest to the gods, and for Aristotle that activity is contemplation. It is through contemplation that we can best resemble the gods because, Aristotle reasoned, the gods are intellectual beings and contemplation is the most perfect activity of the mind. He explains,

> Therefore, the activity of the divinity which surpasses all others in bliss must be a contemplative activity, and the human activity which is most closely akin to it is, therefore, most conducive to happiness. This is further shown by the fact that no other living being has a share in happiness, since they all are completely devoid of this kind of activity. The gods enjoy a life blessed in its entirety; men enjoy it to the extent that they attain something resembling the divine activity; but none of the other living beings can be happy, because they have no share at all in contemplation or study.[28]

What is most striking in Aristotle's reflection is not simply that men and women are happy insofar as they are like the gods, but that there is no other happiness. It is not that the happiness of contemplation is simply relatively greater or more satisfying than some other possible happiness, but, Aristotle hints, it is the only genuine happiness. Aristotle pushes a strong argument, contending there is but one function, one single activity, proper to humankind because only this activity enables happiness. As he sees it, eudaimonia must consist in the contemplative life-which Aristotle takes to be the philosopher's life-and it is in relation to this that all the other virtues must be arranged. That is why Aristotle warns that "we must not follow those who advise us to have human thoughts, since we are only men, and mortal thoughts, as mortals should; on the contrary, we should try to become immortal as far as that is possible and do our utmost to live in accordance with what is highest in us." And the reason this is so, Aristotle concludes, is because even though "this is a small portion of our nature, it far surpasses everything else in power and value. One might even regard it as each man's true self, since it is the controlling and better part."[29]

That last statement is crucial and will be echoed by Aquinas. What Aristotle contends is that human happiness must be linked to contemplative activity since it is only through contemplation that we are given a self most in keeping with who we ought to be. Aristotle does not believe any man or woman can have a fullsome life apart from the intellectual activity of contemplation; rather, it is precisely through the contemplative life that we are formed into a self the very possession of which is our telos, and, therefore, our happiness. For Aristotle it is not the case that we are free to be anything we want to be, nor that competing understandings of self are equally valuable; on the contrary, Aristotle holds there is a self proper to humankind that we do not possess by nature, but a self that is fashioned through the one activity that makes us godlike. It is in assuming this role and undertaking this activity that we gradually gain possession of a self. The message that lingers when the final book of *The Nichomachean Ethics* has been read is that what it means to be human is to be more than human, to resemble, if we can, the gods.

And yet, what frustrated Aristotle, a frustration that is keenly felt in the closing pages of *The Nichomachean Ethics*, is that he had a very hard time understanding how what he saw as so necessary for happiness could be possible. Men and women could be happy, he reasoned, only insofar as they resembled the gods. But how could they possibly become the very creatures they were so unlike? Aristotle considers human nature and is convinced its ultimate perfection resides in a divine life; however, he also admits such a life would be more than human. In fact, Aristotle even counsels that we should never wish this greatest happiness for our friends because then they would be, as gods, so unlike us they could no longer be our friends.

But what Aristotle could not envision, Aquinas could confidently proclaim because Aquinas, shaping a theology informed by grace, could structure his whole understanding of the moral life on the premise that friendship with God is not only possible, but is, indeed, our destiny, absolutely the only thing Christians are called to achieve. What was hoped for but ultimately unthinkable to Aristotle was the core and guiding insight behind all of Thomas's moral theology. If charity is a theological virtue, Thomas suggests, it means we ought to become as much like God as possible, and we can. There is no greater likeness to God than to be God's friend, and friendship with God abides for Thomas as the only adequate description of what the Christian moral pilgrimage is. Therefore, even though Thomas borrowed heavily from Aristotle's analysis of friendship, in charity this friendship has new meaning. Charity takes friendship, as the fundamental teleological activity of our life, to an entirely new level, a level at which, Avital Wohlman suggests, even the most optimistic Aristotle could not reach.[30] Wohlman comments that even though Thomas accepted the structure and explication Aristotle gave friendship, in Aquinas's shaping of charity we are dealing with a wholly other type of friendship, because the fellowship of charity begins not in our desire to be friends with God, but in God's desire to befriend us. It is the gift of God's love to us, Wohlman explains, that both makes possible and begins the friendship we have with God in charity. "Nous sommes décidément loin d'Aristote," she concludes, because unlike Aristotle who focused such friendship in humankind's frustrated straining for the gods, in the friendship of charity, all is reversed: "C'est Dieu qui a l'initiative et tout est suspendu au don indû qu il fait."[31]

Charity is the heart of the Christian life for Aquinas because everything we understand Christianity to be, indeed our very hope, begins in God's overture of friendship to us. As we shall suggest, the moral life is nothing more than receiving and sharing and bringing to perfection this gift of God's love. Thomas is indebted to Aristotle, and our brief study of Aristotle should enable us to appreciate better the force of Aquinas's own insights, but what will be equally clear is that in charity Thomas envisioned a friendship the possibility of which Aristotle could not imagine. The balance of this book will demonstrate that the Christian moral life is nothing more than the ongoing willingness to share in and be formed by the gift of God's love, so that as God's friend we can become as much like God as possible; in fact, it is precisely this sense of the moral life that best helps us appreciate Thomas's treatment of the virtues and their connection to the passions and the Gifts of the Spirit. For now, however, we must consider more carefully what Thomas saw this friendship with God to be.

C. The Good upon which Our Friendship with God is Based

As Richard Egenter points out, every friendship for Thomas is based upon what is communicated or shared between friends because it is this reciprocal sharing in a good that is not only the bond of friendship, but also friendship's activity. Too, a difference in what is communicated or shared accounts for a difference in friendships. Friendships are distinguished in terms of whatever good brings them into being; therefore, in order to know what makes charity as a friendship different from other friendships, we must consider the 'communicatio' upon which it is based.[32] When considering why charity is friendship of a special kind, Aquinas reasons that "the chief concern of any friendship is with the main source of that shared good on which it is based," and notes that

> charity-friendship is based on the sharing of eternal happiness, which consists essentially in God as in its primary source, from which all those capable of eternal happiness derive it. Accordingly, it is God, primarily and above all, who is to be loved in charity, for him we love as the cause of eternal happiness, our neighbor as sharing with us a happiness we both have from God.[33]

It is important to grasp all Thomas discloses in this brief passage because in it he unveils the thrust of his argument for identifying happiness with the friendship we have with God. Simply, Thomas suggests we love whatever makes us happy, and we love most whatever offers us the greatest happiness. What not only causes but also makes possible the special friendship of charity is that God who is perfect happiness offers us a sharing in what accounts for God's happiness; and since we love whatever makes us happy, Thomas says we love God, who is the source of this happiness, as happiness itself.

Aquinas uncovers here several strands in his understanding of happiness. First, he says that in charity not only is God's happiness to be ours, but also that God is our happiness. Aquinas notes that "what communicates happiness to us is lovable because it is the cause of our happiness,"[34] and since God is the cause of our happiness, God is the one in whom our happiness is found. Furthermore, if all our happiness is derived from a sharing in the one who makes us happy, then we are happy to the degree our life is in God. Put simply, since happiness is God, our happiness must be a sharing in or participation in God, and for Thomas this is exactly the meaning of friendship. Charity is friendship because friendship describes the kind of relationship that makes possible intimacy, even union, with the one who is our happiness.

Certainly, what Thomas suggests is entirely in harmony with the opening questions of the *Prima Secundae* when he asks about our final end and concludes God must be our ultimate destiny because "there can be no complete and final happiness for us save in the vision of God."[35] There, however, the reason for Thomas's conclusion is different. When Thomas considers happiness in light of that final end which represents the perfection of happiness because it is the quieting of all desire, the happiness that is found in God appears not so much the principle of all happiness, but simply a more satisfying or complete happiness.[36] It is possible to conclude that one in this world could be genuinely, if not fully happy, apart from God. True, it is not Aquinas's intention to suggest this, but his argument is vulnerable to misinterpretation because there does not yet appear to be any necessary connection between life in God and happiness; rather, the happiness that is found in our final beatitude seems to reside not only at the end of life's journey, but also, to some extent, independently of it.

However, if we compare Aquinas's scrutiny of happiness in the first five questions of the *Prima Secundae* with questions twenty-five and twenty-six in the *Secunda Secundae*, God becomes not only the fullness of happiness, but the principle of happiness. When Thomas thinks about happiness in light of charity, his conclusion is not only that we are most happy in God, but, more pointedly, that we cannot be happy unless we are friends of God.[37] If God is our happiness, to whatever extent we have happiness we must have God. The difference, though subtle, is important because when Thomas thinks of happiness in terms of charity he sees the happiness of God not as something that awaits us at the end of a life of other types of happiness, but as precisely that from which all happiness flows. Here, clearly, Aquinas parallels Aristotle because he argues happiness is not so much a goal of life as it is a function of the activity that most befits us. By identifying happiness with God, Aquinas establishes an unbreakable internal connection between charity-friendship and happiness, contending that the happiness we find in anything, if it is to be real, must flow from happiness we have in God. Charity-friendship is not just the measure of all other happiness, but its source.

But if, as Aquinas suggests, in order to have life we must share God's happiness, we have to know what God's happiness is. Remember, according to Aristotle, happiness is not a condition, but an activity, expressly that activity which corresponds to a thing's proper function. Thomas needs to disclose more carefully exactly in what God's happiness consists, for unless the happiness that bonds our friendship with God is an activity, indeed the core of friendship, it is difficult to speak assuringly of having a friendship at all. In other words, God's happiness cannot be something extrinsic to God, but must be something about the very life of God. It is true that God's happiness is God, but it is hard to know what this means unless we add that God's happiness is the activity that best identifies God, or, as Aristotle would put it, God's happiness is God's proper function. Consequently, to say with Thomas that our life must be a sharing in the happiness of God means the constitutive activity of the Christian, the activity alone which engenders our self, is a partaking in the proper function of God. In this way, human happiness is not a condition that comes from sharing passively in the happiness of God, but is partnership with God in the activity of God's happiness.

Accordingly, as Paul Philippe explains, when Thomas says charity is based on a communication of God's beatitude, we must understand that this beatitude is the identifying perfection of God. Every agent, Philippe reasons, communicates to another the perfection that it has in order to give to the other a form similar to that by which it acts; therefore, when we speak of the perfect Being who is God, what is communicated is God's perfection, the good that God loves and wishes to share with all capable of possessing it. As Philippe writes, "L'amour meut...cet être parfait à causer une similitude de sa perfection dans les autres," that is, "il ne communique pas pour communiquer, mais il agit pour rendre semblable à lui, pour faire communier à sa perfection."[38] Philippe's remarks will take on added force when we consider in detail what it means to be formed in the perfection of God, and how this forming in the perfection of God becomes the essential quality of every virtue, but for now he highlights how we must consider what is communicated in charity. To say that what God shares with us is happiness means the soul of our friendship with God is the offering by God of God's own perfection with the possibility of beholding this perfection not from afar, but of being formed through charity in the goodness and excellence that enables us to be happy as God is happy.

What then is the goodness and perfection of God? Aquinas answers what is best in God is the love or friendship between Father and Son that is Spirit. Just as Aristotle suggests our happiness is our most proper function or activity, so too is God's happiness the friendship which exists between Father and Son, the activity of which is the Spirit. In this sense, Father, Son, and Spirit are one because that Spirit is friendship, and that friendship, as God's proper function and happiness, is the most fitting disclosure of who God is. As Aquinas explains, we have our friendship with God not naturally, but "as infused by the Holy Spirit, who is the love of the Father and the Son; and our participation in this love...is creaturely charity itself."[39]

And this Spirit, who is love, this Spirit who is the friendship between Father and Son, is the gift offered to us in charity that not
only signals the beginning of our life with God,[40] but also indicates
its purpose. Furthermore, if charity is this Gift of the Spirit of the
Father and the Son, then to grow in charity is to be more fully absorbed in the Spirit. As will become evident in the last chapter of
this book when he consider Aquinas's account of the Gifts of the
Spirit, what he pinpoints here is both the task and the fullness of
the Christian moral life. God who desires to be friends with us
shares with us that very friendship by which God is God, that
friendship love between Father and Son that is God's activity, and
therefore, God's happiness. Thus, to say charity is friendship means
we are friends with God to the extent that our friendship with God
is modeled on and becomes the Trinitarian friendship that is God.
And since this friendship is God's happiness, so too shall we be
happy the more the Spirit is our life. Bluntly put, our life and our
happiness come in being friends with God because God is friendship and we who are called to become as much like God as possible
must not only be God's friend, but be God's friend as God is friend.
The goal of our moral life is to have our friendship with God
mirror the friendship who is God. We are to have the same
relationship with God that God, as Trinity, has within God. In a
beautiful passage, Joseph Keller explains:

> Sed insuper in verbis citatis dicit S. Doctor, caritatem esse participationem
> Spiritus Sancti, qui est amor Patris et Filii. Nam sicut omnium operationem
> Dei ad extra prototypon et quasi fons primus absconditus est mysterium Ss.
> Trinitatis secundum processiones divinas ad intra, ita etiam influentiae illius,
> qua Deus communicat nobis beatitudinem suam et diffundit in corda nostra
> amicitiam caritatis, prototypon et quasi fontem reconditum contemplari pos
> sumus in ipsa, ut ita dicam, amicitia divinissima inter Patrem aeternum et
> Filium eius unigenitum quae est ex communicatione unius eiusdemque es
> sentiae divinae, qui amor divinissimae amicitiae est ipse Spiritus Sanctus, qui
> etiam vocatus "nexus" Patris et Filii.[41]

We can begin to see how Thomas has ordered the development
of his moral theology and why, as chapter four will examine, for
him the fullness of charity is the Gifts of the Spirit, that perfection
of friendship when God becomes the active principle of our lives.

Thomas sees the perfection of our friendship with God to be life in the Spirit; in fact, to be possessed by the Spirit is to have achieved the fullness of love. Gift, "as a personal name...is proper to the Holy Spirit," Thomas writes, not just because it is freely given, but moreso because it is through this gift that any other gift proceeds. What Thomas claims is that the Spirit which comes forth as Love is the first and paradigmatic gift, and is also the love in which the fullness of charity is achieved.[42]

But what does Thomas mean by this? And why does he forge such a close connection between charity and the Spirit? A clue is suggested in the very meaning of the word gift. A gift, Thomas suggests, is given only in order that it belong to the one to whom it is given. No one gives a gift in order to take it away, but if it is truly a gift, it is offered that it be possessed fully by the one who receives it, and that is precisely the strategy of charity. God gives us the Spirit in order that we possess that Spirit, or perhaps more aptly, be possessed by it. The strategy implicit in the friendship we have with God is to share so deeply in the Spirit-the life and happiness of God-that we are fully possessed by God, and through that love actually acquire the likeness of God. The Spirit is gift first of all because the fullness of our life, indeed the full meaning of what it is for us to be a self, ultimately is to be transfigured completely in the Spirit. It is this transformation in the Spirit that everything in Thomas's moral theology serves.

Secondly, Thomas contends not only that life in the Spirit is our happiness, but also that we have the power to know and love rightly only insofar as that Spirit is our own.[43] This connection between moral wisdom and the depth of our charity will be explored more fully in chapter four, but for now it is important to see how Thomas establishes a relationship between the capacity for genuine moral goodness and the degree to which our life is absorbed in God. The Spirit is the gift from which all gifts flow, the love that is the source of all love, and our ability to know the good and pursue it, our ability to be truly virtuous at all, is contingent upon our conformity to this gift that is the friendship love of God. For Thomas the Spirit is the law, the New Law that is given through faith in

Christ, because in the Thomistic moral vision the obligation incumbent upon every creature is to be conformed in all their activity to the love and goodness of God.[44] Because the Spirit is the measure of all love and goodness, we, therefore, are able to act rightly insofar as we share in and are configured to this exemplary love of God. The Spirit is the law because God's charity-God's friendship love-is the rule of all goodness; thus, we are good insofar as we live in that love and are ruled by it. Moral goodness is contingent upon our conformity to the Spirit, the full absorption in which is the ongoing work of charity. With profound insight, Thomas explains:

> This, too, is manifest: Just as, to get a body to the place of fire, it must be likened to fire by acquiring that lightness according to which fire is moved by its own motion, so also, to get a man to the beatitude of divine enjoyment which is proper to God in His own nature, these are necessary: first, that by spiritual perfections he be likened to God; then, that he operate with these perfections; and thus, lastly, achieve that beatitude we mentioned. Of course, the spiritual gifts are given to us by the Holy Spirit, as was shown. And thus by the Holy Spirit we are configured to God and through Him we are made ready for good operation. And by the same Spirit the road to beatitude is opened to us.[45]

Obviously Thomas maintains a very close relationship between charity and the Holy Spirit, but does he, like Peter Lombard, identify them, suggesting that "the charity in us by which we love God and our neighbor is nothing more than the Holy Spirit"? Thomas, admitting that Lombard espoused this view out of respect for the excellence of charity, nonetheless concludes it is "ridiculous to say that the very act of love which we express when we love God and our neighbor is the Holy Spirit itself."[46] Thomas wants to distinguish his position from Lombard's because if charity is the Holy Spirit, thereby suggesting the act by which we love God and others is not our own but the Spirit's, then we, who are but instruments of the Spirit, are not the agents of what ought to be our most fitting activity. If Lombard is right it is impossible to speak of charity as a virtue. Aquinas realizes no matter how closely he wants to link charity and the Spirit, he cannot identify them if he is to avoid the awkward conclusion that the act which we take to be an expression of our love for God is not our act at all. If charity is the Holy Spirit, and all acts of love come not from our own agency but only as we are moved by the Spirit, then charity cannot be a virtue because it would not be a voluntary act. If charity is the Spirit, acts of charity belong properly to the Spirit and only instrumentally to us. As Thomas explains:

> For every agent which does not act according to its proper form but only because it is moved by another, is an agent only instrumentally, as an ax is an agent only inasmuch as it is moved by a woodsman. Therefore if the soul does not effect an act of charity through some proper form, but only because it is moved by an extrinsic agent, i.e., by the Holy Spirit, then it will follow that it is considered only as an instrument to this act.[47]

Thomas realizes charity and the Spirit, though intimately connected, must be distinct if charity, precisely as a virtue, is to remain our most fitting and personal activity. On the one hand, Thomas wants to say that fullness in the Spirit is the perfection of charity. But he also wants to say charity is a virtue, and that the love by which we deepen in friendship with God is our own activity. Otherwise, Thomas realizes, he is mired in the unsuitable conclusion that charity is not our act at all. He summarizes:

> Yet, to look at the matter rightly, this rather derogates from charity. The motion of charity springs from the Holy Spirit, but not in such a way that the human mind is passively set in motion and is in no sense the active source of the motion, like a body which is set in motion by an outside force. For this would be incompatible with the very character of a voluntary act, the active principle of which, as shown, lies within the subject itself. Hence a loving choice would not be voluntary, a contradiction in terms, since to be an act of will is of the very nature of human loving. Likewise it cannot be said that the Holy Spirit moves the will as if it were merely an instrument which, although it is the source of its act, has no power of itself to act or not. For this explanation would also destroy the voluntary character of charity, as well as all notion of merit, in spite of the fact that, as shown earlier, the love of charity is the root of merit. It remains that the will must be so moved by the Holy Spirit to the act of love that it must itself also produce it.[48]

And yet, as this passage suggests, although Aquinas wants to distinguish charity and the Spirit, it is a distinction he strains to make. One reason Thomas may want to distance himself so far from Peter Lombard is perhaps because he knows he is vulnerable to the charge that with him charity, despite his insistence, sounds very much like the Spirit. For example, in the passage just cited, Thomas says the "motion of charity springs from the Holy Spirit," but also that every agent is nonetheless "the active source of the motion." Similarly, in *De Caritate*, Aquinas comments: "By this opinion it is not denied that the Holy Spirit, Who is Uncreated Charity, exists in man who has created charity, or that He moves man's soul to the act of love, as God moves all things to their own actions to which they are inclined by their own proper forms."[49] This isn't contradictory, but it is confusing. And, after all, as we shall see in chapter four, Thomas does finally conclude the fullness of the moral life occurs when God becomes the active principle of our lives.

One reason why the precise relationship between charity and the Holy Spirit is not always clear is that sometimes Aquinas does not acknowledge which of two different senses of charity he is using. First, Thomas sometimes refers to charity strictly as a virtue, and here his insistence that charity is something other than the Spirit can be sustained for in each of these cases Thomas focuses not on the perfection of charity, which is the Spirit fully alive in us, but on the agent's activity which makes openness to the Spirit possible. On the other hand, there are times when Aquinas speaks of charity more as the consummation of our friendship with God, the fullness of which is possession of the Spirit.

Thus, Aquinas distinguishes two senses of charity, one as the virtue expressive of our active friendship with God, the other as the Spirit, expressive of that friendship's perfection. In this sense, charity can be said to be the Spirit insofar as the Spirit is the harvest of our friendship with God. But exactly that understanding of charity demands a corresponding account of charity as a virtue, the ongoing activity of a life spent in friendship with God that makes life in the Spirit possible. To harvest the Spirit requires a life given to careful cultivation of friendship with God. The Spirit is our perfect possession of the happiness of God, but to gain this requires the onerous, stubborn transformation of our life, and that is the work of charity as a virtue. The Spirit is the happiness of God, and to be possessed by that happiness is charity's greatest possibility, as well as its most proper function.

D. Why Our Happiness is Charity-Friendship with God

To suggest that charity is a virtue whose perfection is the Spirit, and that this perfect lovelife with God is our happiness, is to remember from Aristotle that happiness is an activity; therefore, to share God's happiness is to participate in the activity that is most properly God's. Drawing upon Aristotle, what Aquinas does is suggest God's happiness is our happiness exactly because God's most proper activity and our most proper activity are, in one sense, the same. Like Aristotle, Thomas reaches this conclusion first by contending that human happiness is an activity. Secondly, like Aristotle, Thomas forges an internal connection between this activity and our telos to demonstrate that human perfection, though not yet fully achieved by this activity, is nonetheless intrinsic to it. In this way, Thomas not only protects Aristotle's link between the virtues and eudaimonia, but also gives the activity that is happiness a more historical edge by suggesting that while happiness displays that "each thing is perfect inasmuch as it is actual" so that "happiness...must go with man's culminating actuality," the term or perfection of happiness refers to "the full development of what has already begun to live."[50]

What is the activity of our happiness? We know the activity that accounts for our happiness must be our best activity, "that is to say when our highest power is engaged with its highest object," which is God. How is this so? Following Aristotle, Aquinas says "the activity of contemplating the things of God" is our "principal happiness" because through contemplation we are brought "into converse with the highest beings, namely with God and the angels," and thus made like them in happiness.[51] To contemplate God is to be in perfect fellowship with God. Thus, Aquinas's sense of contemplation, in at least one important way, is different from Aristotle's. Aristotle said contemplation was our highest virtue not because it joined us to the gods, but because since the gods were essentially intellectual beings, intellectual activity, such as contemplation, was the way we, though remote from the gods, could most resemble them. Aquinas, however, speaks of contemplation as the activity of beholding God by being with God. To see God and be absorbed in the presence of God is our highest activity. In this way, contemplation, instead of being an activity other than friendship, is its most powerful expression because to contemplate God is to be thoroughly and actively joined to God. That is why even though Thomas describes contemplation as an act of the mind, it is not opposed to charity but is, indeed, the result of charity. Contemplation is a nearness to God made possible by charity. To be forever in the presence of God, which is what contemplation involves, is exactly what charity desires and what a life of charity achieves.

And yet, as historical beings making their way to God, we cannot be perfectly happy because we cannot yet sustain the activity of a perfect contemplative union with God. Happiness is the activity commensurate with our best and highest function, which Thomas says is contemplation, but because we are human a perfectly contemplative life is not possible for us. We cannot survive through the practice of a single activity, however noble. As human, multiple activities are demanded of us. Thus, Thomas compares but also distinguishes our happiness and God's. God's happiness is the measure for our own, but we cannot, like God, be wholly absorbed in one activity. We are called to cleave to God through contemplative love, but the various demands of our human condition make it impossible for that to be the only activity in which we are involved. What will be the case in the Kingdom of God cannot possibly be so here. As Aquinas explains,

> Final perfection for men in their present life is their cleaving to God by activity which, however, cannot be continuous or consequently single, for activity becomes multiple when interrupted. That is why we cannot possess perfect happiness now, as Aristotle admits; after a long discussion of the sort of happiness men can reach, he concludes, "We call them happy, but only as men." God, however, promises us complete happiness, when we shall be as the angels in heaven.[52]

The ever greater focusing of our activity on God is the work of charity, and that explains why contemplating God unrestrictedly might be the perfection of our happiness, but as the perfection of happiness is itself an activity of friendship. The problem with

Thomas's isolation of contemplation as the most proper activity of happiness is that it is not always seen to have a connection with charity. At times contemplation appears to be an activity not only independent of charity-friendship with God, but also something other than that friendship. But that cannot be the case for the very intimacy with God Thomas explains contemplation to be is possible only on the basis of the friendship life a Christian has with God. In this way, there is no separation between the activity of charity-friendship and the activity of contemplation because contemplation is but the form the life of charity finally takes.

Nonetheless, the problem with pinpointing contemplation as our highest and most perfect activity, especially if it is not acknowledged that contemplation takes its meaning from charity and is expressive of that, is that contemplation may imply a passivity that does not adequately express that our happiness is a function of our friendship with God. In short, it is just that element of relatedness that is crucial to Aquinas's understanding of beatitude, a perfection of happiness that includes contemplation, but is essentially the fullness of friendship. As we shall see, the very thing Thomas wants to argue about charity is that friendship with God is our happiness because beatitude requires not just beholding God, but being continually related to God in a colloquy of love.

That is why it is more proper to focus on the relationship Thomas establishes between charity and beatitude. Beatitude is not something different from charity, but is the activity of charity perfectly realized. True, charity as friendship prepares for beatitude and makes it possible, but the internal correspondence Aquinas creates between our activity and our happiness can never be severed. Charity is beatitude because friendship with God is our most proper activity, and, therefore, our happiness. Conversely, beatitude is charity inasmuch that perfect happiness must be the uninterrupted and complete activity of a friendship in which God and we are one. As Guindon aptly writes, "Non seulement béatitudé et charite ne s'opposent pas dans la pensée saint Thomas: elles sont corrélatives comme l'objet poursuivi et la puissance qui nous y fait tendre, comme le terme et le principe d'un mouvement."[53] The activity of charity then not only is our happiness, but deepens that happiness by allowing us to inhere more wholly in God. The Aristotelian influence on Thomas is clear because charity is not the activity that prepares for beatitude, but is, rather, the activity that both contains within itself and realizes our telos.

Implicit in the relationship Aquinas establishes between charity and beatitude is his awareness that happiness is not something the very desire of which makes possible its possession, but is a function of particular ways of life undertaken and adhered to as good. Happiness is internally connected to various ways of life because it is mediated as the activities and practices of those manners of living are claimed as our own. As Guindon so rightly explains, "En conséquence, pour participer à une félicité quelconque, il faut qu'on prenne part à la vie dont cette félicité est la perfection." Therefore, he argues, if perfect happiness is to be possible for us, "il apparaît qu'il nous faut tout d'abord participer à la vie divine. Or c'est précisément l'amitié qui, par-dessus tout, réalise la communauté de vie dont nous parlons."[54] Guindon's point is that if happiness is contingent upon participating in whatever manner of life is constitutive of a particular happiness, then having the happiness of God requires seeing our life to be an ongoing participation in the life of God.

Furthermore, this sharing in the life of God must be understood as radically as possible. It is not a sharing that enables our person to be unchanged. Indeed, as Horvath explains, to participate through charity in the life of God is to share so fully in that life and to make ourselves so vulnerable to it that our life really is no longer our own. Horvath says the friendship of charity implies the highest form of participation between God and ourselves, and thus we do not so much "take part" (Teil-nahme) in the life of God, but take that life on (Ganz-nahme) as the norm and standard of our own. In charity we succumb so wholly to the life of God that one kind of life and one way of being a self is replaced by another. To participate in the life of God through charity means we pledge to share so fully in that life that we are gradually conformed to it.[55] Thus, if we have come to see God's life as our own, perfect conformity to that life makes perfect happiness possible.

That happiness requires sharing a way of life reflects Thomas's teaching that selfhood is gained through participation.[56] As Albert Ilien explains in his study of the Thomistic theory of love, *Wesen und Funktion Der Liebe bei Thomas von Aquin*, only God is happy, good and lovable "per essentiam suam;" therefore, men and women can be happy in the measure they share the life of God. Ilien's point is not only that we cannot be happy apart from God, but more strikingly that we cannot even have life apart from God. For Aquinas, we have both happiness and life not in ourselves, but only insofar as we stand in relationship with God. Thus, friendship with God not only is, but has to be our life; it must be the most comprehensive description we give ourselves because only in that relationship is life, selfhood, and happiness possible. Apart from God we are nothing because we who have life from God are not capable of engendering it ourselves; rather, our life and our happiness are bestowed, and they come to us insofar as we stand in a relationship which enables us to receive them. Friendship with God is the relationship which best enables us to receive life from God. As Ilien says, "Die 'beatitudo' des Menschen nur in einer Teil-Nahme am gottlichen Sein bestehen: 'Homines...sunt beati...per participationem' (I-II 3, 1 ad 1)." Too, like Horvath, Ilien insists that if our life comes only as we share in the life of God, this sharing must not only make God present to us, but also be the love activity by which we gain likeness to God, for our possibility for union with God is in proportion to our likeness to God. Consequently, we have life, and indeed a self, the more our friendship with God makes us like God. As Ilien concludes, "Diese 'participatio', 'adeptio', 'possessio' oder 'fruitio' ist zugleich eine Verähnlichung ('assimilatio') mit Gott, ja eine 'coniunctio cum Deo'."[57]

From a more philosophical perspective, Robert Johann's *The Meaning of Love* offers a helpful way of appreciating the crucial importance of charity in the moral life. The relationship Thomas forges between charity and beatitude reflects what Johann calls Aquinas's "metaphysics of participation,"[58] and captures the genius behind Thomas's insistence that charity is most fittingly understood as friendship. Johann says life must be a friendship with God and this must be the relationship from which all others originate because God is the One from whom all else is. Aquinas's "metaphysics of participation" signifies "there is always a distinction in creatures between themselves as actual and that by which they are actual," and since God, as Johann puts it, is "pure actuality Himself, He is also the source of all actuality in creatures," and as that source is the One by whom "they are rendered actual and perfect."[59]

Using slightly different language, Johann is once more displaying why the moral life must be the ongoing saga of our friendship with God. All life, all being and goodness, emerge from participation in the life of God, and this is exactly what the friendship of charity renders. Friendship with God is our life because outside that relationship we are not simply different, we are nothing. Johann's point is that we exist only insofar as we 'ex-ist', that is, have life in and from God and not from ourselves; and we are most susceptible to such 'ex-istence' when our relationship to God is one of friendship. It is this relationship that is the most crucial activity from which our self is drawn. In other words, to be a self is to be a friend of God. Johann writes:

> That is why a man becomes himself only in existing more intensely, only in suspending his life from values that surpass the narrow limits of his own existence-and this does not mean the effacement of the I before an impersonal ideal, but on the contrary an adhesion that is eminently personal to the Source of all personality. I establish myself in existence only in the measure that I turn myself towards God and situate myself before his eyes.[60]

And if it is true that God is the good by which we are perfected, the One by whom every human being discovers and achieves his or her intended expression, then a metaphysics of participation becomes a metaphysics of assimilation as well. As Johann explains, "[N]othing will be good and desirable except insofar as it participates in the likeness of God, each creature, in desiring that by which it is perfected, is at the same time seeking a similitude of the divine perfection and goodness."[61]

What does this mean? Perhaps not only that friendship with God gives us ourself, but more precisely that the very activity of friendship with God is ourself. If charity is friendship and friendship is beatitude, then the Christian's self is not something derived from friendship, nor the residue of friendship, but is the life of friendship with God wholeheartedly undertaken. If our self is our friendship with God, then selfhood persists only as this activity is sustained through loving both God and all those dear to God. That is why Johann says charity teaches us what we really love in our self, indeed, the true value of ourself, is nothing innate to us as human beings, but our capacity to live in love with God and neighbor. Our dignity is that we can befriend all things good.[62]

Johann's analysis enables us to see more clearly why happiness is a friendship we have with God that reaches its perfection in the Spirit. If charity-friendship is the condition for the possibility of being at all, then happiness resides in our full assimilation to God, a fullness best described as life in the Spirit. Thus, the Christian moral life is a life of friendship with God for it is in the measure that we acquire likeness to God through charity's love that we also acquire a self.

That charity-friendship with God is the beginning and end of the Christian life, its most proper activity as well as its telos, explains why charity is the key to understanding Thomas's account of the virtues. In short, that charity is a friendship love through which men and women continually acquire a likeness to God not only indicates why for Thomas the virtues cannot be considered apart from the passions, particularly love, but also why the virtues reach their fullness in the Gifts. The argument of this book is that the importance Thomas places on charity in his account of the Christian moral life indicates why it is in light of this transforming friendship with God that his ethic of virtue is best understood. Consequently, if we are to appreciate how charity is central to understanding the *Prima Secundae*, we must consider in more detail the three qualities Thomas says constitute friendship, especially when the friend we love is God.

E. The Elements of Friendship Once More Considered

What makes friendship a different sort of love is that the focus of its love is not one's self, but the other. Friendship reverses the direction of love's concern for unlike a love of pleasure or utility, in friendship the good immediately desired is not one's own, but the friend's. This is the meaning of benevolence, the first mark of friendship. As Neveut explains, with friendship the 'penchant' or thrust of the love is different because in loving one's friend and seeing the friend as another self, the good that is love's interest is not the pleasure or usefulness that accrues to the one who loves, but the good of the friend herself.[63] What qualifies any love as friendship is that the strategy of friendship is to discover one's own good not by directly seeking it, but by discovering it through devotion to the good of another.

This is exactly the attack Thomas uses in singling out what makes friendship love a different kind of love. Thomas, following Aristotle, says all love "consists in wanting good things for someone....The movement of love therefore has a two-fold object: the good thing which is wanted for someone, whether oneself or another person, and the one for whom it is wanted. The former is the object of love-of-desire; the latter is the object of love-of-friendship."[64] All loves share a desire for a particular good, but what distinguishes loves is the one for whom the good is desired and the reason it is desired. Friendship is a love that toils for the good of the other. It is a love whose very activity seeks to cultivate the well-being and flourishing of the other not because the one who loves has no good of his own, but because what he loves and sees as his good is precisely the good of the friend.

Benevolence implies not only that the friend is loved for herself, but also that because she is loved the active seeking of her good is the sustaining project of the lover's life. To love from benevolence means not just that one hopes for the good of another, but that the one who loves consecrates all his energy to seeking and upholding the good of his friend. Friendship describes a life given to promoting the good of the friend, and this is undertaken joyfully and eagerly because being a friend of this particular person is viewed as one of the most important projects of one's life.[65]

And yet, there must be something more to friendship than this because the devotion benevolence implies, if it is not returned, can be enervating and disappointing. There is nothing sadder than to be devoted to someone who fails to appreciate our love or refuses to return it. Similarly, there is nothing more disheartening than to feel the kindness given by another is but a ploy to keep our affections at bay. Good will is necessary for friendship, but it is not sufficient. In addition to benevolence, friendship requires mutual affection between the friends; in short, the well-wishing requisite for friendship must be matched by a warmth and affection that each friend has for the other. Thomas speaks of this as "a certain affective union between lover and beloved, inasmuch as the lover, seeing the beloved as one with himself or as part of him, is thereby attracted." What distinguishes this from benevolence is that benevolence "is a simple act of the will, which makes us wish another well without presupposing any such union," but friendship "includes goodwill, but adds to it a union of the affections."[66]

It is important to understand exactly what Thomas is saying. Benevolence is a necessary part of friendship, but friendship demands more than just good will. The cost of friendship is the gift of ourself, the ongoing willingness to offer ourself to another, to be vulnerable to her invitation to affirm her life as good by our willingness to become part of it. Friendship demands more than benevolence; indeed, Aquinas suggests, it demands the extraordinary risk of seeing the other as another self. And so when Aquinas remarks that to be friendship, benevolence must be accompanied by a "certain affective union," he is speaking of the costliest union possible because mutual affection signals not only agreement in what is good, but also, as Pépin says, the willingness to allow ourselves to become part of another.[67] Here Thomas follows Aristotle who knew that while "good will is the beginning of friendship," to be friendship truly it must be accompanied by mutual affection.[68] But what makes Thomas's use of Aristotle portentous is that he applies it to charity, and that means friendship with God requires not only that we wish for God's good, but that we also are willing to suffer the possibility of being of one heart with God.

This second mark of friendship is reciprocity. Friendship is a relationship, and as a relationship it is constituted by the good will and affection that is exchanged between friends, the mutual delighting in which is friendship's express activity. That is why Aristotle says it is silly to talk of having friendship with a bottle of wine or even a horse because friendship exists only where the good will we have for another is consciously and intentionally reciprocated.[69] Thus, friendship, strictly speaking, exists only when the good will we feel toward another is felt toward us. As Johann writes:

> For friendship, it is not sufficient to love another directly as myself; to be friendship, my love of benevolence must be explicit reciprocated. Friendship exists only between those who love one another. Thus it is conceived as adding to a one-sided love of benevolence a certain society of lover and beloved in their love.[70]

Johann's last comment is telling first because it underscores the obvious fact that for friendship there must not only be another to whom we can be a friend, but also another who reciprocates our friendship by desiring what is good for us as we do for her. Secondly, Johann's remark suggests this mutual love which exists between friends, this ongoing exchange of shared and cherished values, reveals friendship to be a type of 'society' or fellowship, a miniature community of sorts, in which those who are friends are bonded together by a common love. The very meaning of friendship suggests it is more than the grouping of people who care for each other; rather, friendship is the society established and sustained by those who mutually enrich each other because they are nurtured from the same goods. In this sense, friends are able to wish for one another's good because the good they desire for the other is the good both share, the flourishing in which is the activity of friendship itself.

In his classic study, *Le Rôle De L'Amitié Dans La Vie Chretiénne Selon S. Thomas,* Paul Philippe pushes this argument further. He explains that friendship demands contact with the other who is our friend initially because the only way we know someone is our friend is if through his presence we have become aware of his concern for us. But friendship is more than that. Friendship is not only the relation of those who mutually care for one another, but is, as Philippe says, "un commerce vital, une certaine vie sociale, une 'communicatio' des personnes."[71] Philippe's point is that a relationship in which people mutually care for each other and wish for one another's good is only minimally a friendship because friendship, properly speaking, is a relationship or society that is formed through the active exchange of a good. When Philippe writes that "toute amitié est fondée sur une sociétié, sur une communication vitale,"[72] he means not only that friendship is the active, mutual nurturing in the good which bonds the friends, but also that the sharing and participation in this good is friendship's rationale. In a certain sense, friendships are formed not so much because others first make known their concern for us, but because others, in sharing our values, are uniquely able to wish for our good. Thus, friendship is not as much a choice as it is a discovery, not so much the constructing of a relationship as the emergence of one.

This is the logic behind Aristotle's remark that friends who never spend time together do not stay friends for long. As simple as that sounds, Aristotle's reflection betrays a profound insight. If by definition friendship is a society, the very meaning of which is the ongoing nurturing of a shared good, then there must be a way that friends share life together. Aristotle puts this even stronger by arguing that "those who extend friendship to one another without living together are more like men of good will than like friends. For nothing characterizes friends as much as living in each other's company."[73] It is true that we often do remain friends with people we seldom see, but the force of Aristotle's comment cannot be overlooked. The test of any friendship is our willingness to let our life be shaped by it, not only to spend time with our friend and be present to her, but also to succumb to the friendship, to make ourself vulnerable to it because in some way our life is created from it. And so when Aristotle says that friends are those who "spend their days together" and "find joy in one another,"[74] he means not just that

friends are happy to be together, but that the society their friendship forms is their happiness.

By the end of *The Nichomachean Ethics*, one has the impression
that for Aristotle ethics is no longer a function of politics, but of
friendship. Or perhaps that society's most crucial polity is character
friendships because friendships based on a love for virtue are the
communities which best enable people to be good. As Aristotle
asks: "Is it...true of friends that the most desirable thing for them is
to live together?" Yes, "friends aim at living together" because
"whatever his existence means to each partner individually or
whatever is the purpose that makes his life desirable, he wishes to
pursue it together with his friends." Why? Because "whatever each
group of people loves most in life, in that activity they spend their
days together. For since they wish to live together with their
friends, they follow and share in those pursuits which, they think,
constitute their life together."[75]   In short, friendship is a society
among those who agree on what is good, and as a society it is the
activity constitutive of both the life and the person of the friend.
We need to be with our friends not just because we wish to share
our good with them, but, more emphatically, because we need
them in order to be endowed with our good at all. Friendship is the
constitutive activity of our life because through it we come in touch
with the goods most crucial to who we are and hope to become.

Once more, Aristotle's analysis is helpful for understanding how
Aquinas perceived the partnership of charity. In his *Scriptum Super
Sententiis Magistri Petri Lombardi*, Aquinas speaks of friendship as
a "societas quaedam amantis et amati in amore," and of charity
specifically as a "quaedam amicitia hominis ad Deum, per quam
homo Deum diligit et Deus hominem; et sic efficitur quaedam as-
sociatio hominis ad Deum, ut dicitur I Joan., I,7: 'Si in luce ambu-
lamus, sicut et ipse in luce est, societatem habemus ad invicem.'"[76]
Friendship is the society or partnership of two who participate in
the same love, and from that participation discover themselves
friends. They are lover and beloved for one another because they
are nourished by the same good, and their friendship is a society in
that good. Accordingly, charity represents not just that God loves

us and we love God, but more truly the 'society' or 'association' we have with God and God with us because of the good which bonds us together. Charity is the ongoing delighting with God in the good both God and we love.

In that same passage from Aquinas's commentary on the *Sentences*, he cites Aristotle's description of friendship as a 'conversation' with our friend in what we both love and consider to be our life. The 'convivere' or life together of the friends is fittingly understood as the ongoing 'conversation' they have about the goods they love. The 'conversing' in the good that is the life of friendship makes possible a conversion to the good that is the hope of friendship.

But what is striking about Thomas's reference to friendship as a 'conversation' in the good is that he applies it to charity. The friendship we have with God, he says, must be understood as a coming together with God, a 'convivere' or 'conversare' over a good we share with God.[77] To understand charity as friendship is to see it as the society or partnership with God that is sustained by the mutual and lasting 'communication' of the same good. To the degree that we 'converse' in or turn toward the good we love, we are finally made one with it. But such union and, therefore, genuine conversion, does not precede charity, but is its harvest. Conversion to God is a measure of the friendship we have with God, not its condition. In this sense, conversion is the work of virtues formed from charity not just because turning to God takes time, but more exactly because it is the harvest of love and the achievement of friendship.

Interestingly, this 'convivere' or life together of which Aquinas speaks was, early in this century, the locus of a dispute over the Thomistic meaning of friendship. In his 1906 *Revue Thomiste* article, M. Coconnier argued that the 'communicatio' of which Aquinas speaks when he discusses that upon which charity is based, is this commerce or partnership, the actual life-together in which the goods formative of friendship are exchanged. For Coconnier, what is communicated in charity is not beatitude, but the 'convivere', the social commerce itself.[78]

In response, Tibor Horvath charges that Conconnier, by arguing that the 'convivere' and the 'communicatio' of charity are the same, implies, contrary to Aquinas, that the basis of friendship is not the common possession of a good, but the 'gemeinschaft' of friendship itself.[79] If this is what Conconnier meant, he clearly misinterpreted Thomas. As we have shown, Thomas expressly says what is communicated in charity as the basis of our friendship with God is God's beatitude, the sharing and delighting in which effects the society of friends. In their article, "La Charité Comme Amitié D'Après S. Thomas," Joseph Keller and Benoit Lavaud say that while Thomas saw a life in common as a necessary part of friendship, following Aristotle, he realized it could not be the constitutive element of friendship. For example, even though soldiers and sailors share a common life, a life that may look very much like friendship, they are not necessarily friends. Agreement on what is good is what brings friendship to life, and while flourishing in this good demands the society of friends, their life together does not precede but is consequent to the good they share. As Keller and Lavaud explain:

> Tous ceux qui ont ces relations ne deviennent pas amis, mais seulement ceux à qui elles agréent, parce qu'ils s'y découvrent des affinités, des sympathies, des convenances, des accords: Le vrai fondement de l'amitié doit donc être cherché jusque dans ces affinites.[80]

Similarly, Egenter notes that Thomas speaks of friendship as effecting or producing a life together, even as demanding it, but that is only because of the good which precedes it:

> Der übernatürliche Verkehr der Seele mit Gott, das 'convivere', kann der Freundschaft nicht vorausgehen, sondern folgt ihr, wie gerade der oben angeführte Text, der für die Gottesfreundschaft die Teilnahme am göttlichen Leben erfordert, dartut. Dort spricht Thomas davon, dass die Freundschaft das Zusammenleben bewirke (facit), und dass wir durch die Freundschaft (qua sibi conviveremus) mit den Freunden zusammenleben.[81]

In criticizing Conconnier's interpretation of the 'communication' which founds friendship, neither Keller nor Lavaud nor Egenter wants to deny that a life together is requisite for the activity of friendship; they only want to position it properly. As Keller and Lavaud explain, even though this social commerce does not establish friendship, it is necessary if friendship is to achieve its purpose of sustaining a conversation with the good. In relating this to charity, they write:

> S'il s'agit de l'amitié divine, laquelle n'est pas acquise, mais infuse, le commerce ne la fonde pas, car il n'est établi que par elle; mais il favorise sa croissance: plus l'âme chrétienne vit et 'converse', a commerce intime avec Dieu, plus elle lui devient semblable et plus elle expérimente sa douceur.[82]

Or, as Egenter explains, even though this 'social Verkehr' is not the basis of friendship, it is the proper act of friendship and, as that activity, represents the dynamic toward union that is friendship's most pressing concern:

> Jede Liebe zieht ja nach sich das Streben nach einer realen Gegenwart des Geliebten. Thomas selbst hat ganz klar das Streben nach dem Zusammenleben zurückgeführt auf den der Liebe allgemein innewohnenden Drang nach realer Vereinigung und es somit als Folgeerscheinung der Liebe dargetan.[83]

And yet, while their criticisms are helpful in distinguishing and ordering the various elements Thomas saw in friendship, perhaps Keller and Lavaud and Egenter are not entirely fair in their criticisms of Coconnier. In his much disputed article of 1906, Coconnier defines the 'communicatio' of charity thusly: "C'est l'avoir en commun de certaines choses, dont on jouit à titre égal, dans une fréquentation assidue, dans un vivre ensemble continuel, dans l'intimité constante d'une vie toute à deux."[84] Coconnier may not delineate clearly enough that the basis of friendship is the good in which the friends take mutual delight and not, at least principally, the common life through which this delight is enjoyed; nonetheless, it seems Coconnier has not been read carefully enough. He acknowledges the difference between the goods which are communicated in friendship and the relationship necessary if those goods are to be shared. Where Keller and Lavaud and Egenter seem unfair in their criticisms of Coconnier is that when citing the passage in which Coconnier does indeed say that "pour saint Thomas, en matière d'amitié, la 'communicatio' et le 'convivere' signifient, au fond, la même chose," they fail to cite the rest of that passage in which Coconnier says that even though the 'communicatio' and the 'convivere' represent the same thing, they "marquent une simple différence de point de vue." In other words, they signify the same thing, the same reality, but only insofar as one realizes it is friendship viewed from two different perspectives.

Coconnier explains this clearly. In the very next sentence he writes: "'Communicatio' signifie l'avoir en commun de certains biens, de certaines réalitiés, constituant l'objet et comme la base d'un commerce social," and Keller, Lavaud, and Egenter would surely agree with this. He continues: "Et 'convivere' signifie un commerce social ayant pour base ou pour objet l'avoir en commun de certains biens, de certaines réalitiés." How does this differ from his critics? All Coconnier says is that "la 'communicatio' est l'acte initial dont le 'convivere' n'est que le prolongement,"[85] and in this he not only faithfully interprets Aquinas, but stands in surprising agreement with his critics. What they fail to see is that with this final distinction between the 'communicatio' of certain goods that is the initial act of friendship and the 'convivere' that is its prolongation, Coconnier acknowledges that the communication upon which friendship is based is conceptually distinct from the life activity which sustains it. Moreover, he seems to be right that when viewed as a whole both the "communication" of the good of friendship and the sharing of this good comprise one reality, though seen from different perspectives. More importantly, the value of Coconnier's emphasis on the 'convivere' of friendship is that it underscores the necessity of friends being together if friendship's most important task, that of coming to see the friend as another self, can be achieved. It is this third mark of friendship we must now consider.

In Book Three of his *Summa Contra Gentiles*, Aquinas remarks that "the ultimate end of things is to become like God," and this happens insofar as "created things...attain to divine goodness."[86] Exactly this, I think, is the strategy behind Aquinas's definition of charity as friendship since it is in friendship with God that we become more like God. What our study of charity has shown us is that if becoming a Christian is to become as much like God as possible, then charity, as a life of friendship with God, is precisely the activity through which we come to resemble God. For Thomas, the intimacy with God that accrues through charity is not simply closeness to God, but an intimacy of being and character, an intimacy of virtue and goodness, that allows us the staggering possibility of beholding God as another self. We said before that the goal of every friendship is union with the one we love; however, union is an expression of the most radical, intimate kinship, that of being one with another because we see him or her as not only like us, but so much a part of who we are that he or she is for us another self.

That this is possible between God and ourselves is Aquinas's claim about charity. Charity is the virtue whose work is to make us as much like God as possible for the very reason that we are ourselves in the measure that we participate in God. Coming to see God as another self signals not a loss of self, but the achievement of self because if being a self requires being in God, then the fullness and perfection of every self occurs when our life is so much formed by God and in God that we look upon God as another self. The change this requires of us is monumental, perhaps frightening, but Aquinas's point is that such a change, effected through charity, is required of us if we are to achieve Christianity's promise. Charity is the virtue that works us through this change, slowly reshaping us from people who are strangers to God into people who call God friend. To become another self to God is the almost blasphemous promise of charity. As Keller writes, when that occurs we have a friendship unrivaled in beauty or intimacy or happiness:

> Ex ista autem inter Deum et hominem deiformem intima vitae similitudine et communione enascitur amicitia inter Deum et hominem, secundum quam Deus gloriosus hominem et homo deiformis Deum apprehendit et aestimat ut quasi idem sibi seu alterum seipsum et invicem sibi volunt bonum sicut sibimetipsis, societate quadam mirabili amoris invicem amantes atque amando dantes invicem seipsos. Quae utique intelligenda sunt prout conveniunt amicitiae quae dicitur superexcellentiae et proportionalitatis; nihilominus tamen nulla inter homines unio amicabilis etiam amicitiae aequalitatis tam est intima, quam illa amicitia divina superexcellentiae, quia nulla inter

homines vitae similitudo et communio potest esse tam intima, quam est inter Deum et hominem in communicatione qua Deus suam beatitudine seu vitam propriam communicat homini.[87]

For Aquinas, what makes this union of selves possible is that love both expresses and works toward a similitude between the lover and the loved one. Specifically, charity is the love whereby we become similar to the God who is love, and this similitude is the basis of our capacity to see God as another self. In short, there is a direct correspondence between beholding God as another self and the similitude with God caused by charity. Through charity we come to see God as another self because through that friendship love the lover becomes similar to the one who is loved.

In his article, "L'Amitié De La Charité," Henri Noble says this similarity between friends is first experienced as "une similitude de pensées, de sentiments, de rêves, d'idéals....Nous reconnaissons dans quelqu'un à travers un signe, une expression, un mot, les mêmes manières de voir, les mêmes goûts, les mêmes aspirations."[88] But friendship pushes toward a deeper similitude, a resemblance not just in tastes and interests, even in values and convictions, but a similarity so deep that "nous vivons l'un avec l'autre et l'un par l'autre; nous ne faisons qu'un cœur et qu'une âme."[89] Noble's point is that the resemblance intended by charity is the deepest kind for it is a resemblance of self. To see the friend as another self, and to consider ourselves but a reflection of the friend, is the similitude toward which friendship strains. It is a similitude so penetrating that the friends become one, that one is for the other exactly what the other is for himself.

Remember, however, that Aquinas makes the same claim about charity. Charity's charge is to make us so much like God that our intimacy with God turns on our likeness to the goodness of God. Certainly this likeness is never complete-it describes the never ending activity of beatitude-but it is, nonetheless, a claim Thomas makes about the capacity of our life with God. Friendship fashions a relationship with God in which by sharing the very form of God we come to be for God who God is for us, a friend, a lover, another self. Charity pushes for a similitude to God that stops at nothing short of perfect union with God, a kinship so intimate that it manifests itself as Spirit. That is why Keller and Lavaud insist that to understand what charity promises we must understand precisely the kind of similitude Thomas proposes:

> Du reste ce n'est pas n'importe quelle ressemblance qui peut servir de base à l'amitié. Une ressemblance purement physique et toute secondaire dans les traits du visage ou le teint, par exemple, ne saurait évidemment pas suffire. Il faut une ressemblance qui permette à chacun de voir dans l'autre un autre soi-même: c'est-à-dire une ressemblance foncière, en un domaine estimé principal, en des choses qui touchent de près à la personne-sous un certain rapport, ou absolument, une ressemblance en ce qui définit une vie, lui donne son orientation, sa forme, ressemblance par conséquent en ce qui concerne la fin, qu'il s'agisse de la fin dernière ou d'une fin subordonnée, comme celle que poursuivent en commun les membres des mêmes sociétés.[90]

Both H.D. Simonin and Richard Egenter argue that the kind of similitude necessary for one person to see another as her or his self is a similitude of being. Simonin, for example, says Thomas has in mind an actual "similtude ontologique" when he speaks of the resemblance charity effects between God and ourself,[91] and Egenter elaborates that this similtude of being (Ähnlichkeit Des Seins) is both the effective cause and sustaining principle of friendship.[92] Simonin and Egenter are groping to express Thomas's premise that charity works to make us as much like God as possible, and surely there is no greater likeness than the ontological similitude they propose.

But the danger in their position, Horvath cautions, is to infer that we become so much like God that we are no longer different from God. What has to be guarded against in speaking of the similitude fashioned by charity as ontological is the suggestion that in becoming so much like God we are no longer other than God. Simonin and Egenter are right to press as fully as possible Aquinas's insistence that through charity we come to regard God as another Self, and there is a way that 'ontological similitude' aptly conveys what this means; however, it is also vulnerable to the conclusion that there is then no longer any difference between God and ourselves. To say that charity makes us as much like God as possible is not to say that God is no longer someone other, but that we exist fully and most properly as a self insofar as we participate ever more deeply in God. To recognize God as another self is not to identify God and the self, but to recognize that God is the one by whom we always are.

That is why Horvath describes the similitude effected by charity differently. "In dem geliebten Gegenstand findet der Liebende nicht sich selbst, sondern er findet den Geliebten, wie sich selbst. Thomas vergleicht, aber er identifiziert nicht."[93] This is a very important distinction and is not liable, like Simonin's and Egenter's ontological similitude, of possibly identifying God and the self. Horvath's point is that the similitude wrought by charity means not that God is identical to ourself, but that through friendship with God we grow in likeness to God. In other words, the likeness to God wrought by charity does not mean there is no longer any difference between God and ourselves; rather, it means God can be considered another self to us because through friendship love we have become godly. The similitude Aquinas speaks about, as chapter two will make clear, is a similitude of form; however, to share the form of God does not mean we are God, but that in being ourself we must be God's friends.[94]

What it means in charity to call God friend, why that friendship is our happiness, and how growing in friendship with God is the project of the Christian moral life has been the focus of chapter one. In many ways, this is the most critical chapter of our study because if we are to show that Aquinas's treatment of the passions, the virtues, and the Gifts is best understood in light of the prominence he gives charity, then we have to understand clearly what for Thomas being a friend of God means. The argument of this chapter is that if our perfection, and, therefore, our happiness, resides in our sharing the life of God, and if such participation in God is rendered best through a friendship whose love gradually makes us like God, then the moral theology of the *Prima Secundae* is most helpfully interpreted in light of charity. How this might give a fuller reading of Thomas's treatise on the passions, and why it is in light of them that the virtues are best understood, is the subject of chapter two.

Notes

1 Tibor Horvath, *Caritas Est In Ratione* (Münster: Aschendorff, 1966); Albert Ilien, *Wesen und Funktion der Liebe bei Thomas von Aquin* (Freiburg:Herder, 1975).

2 Aquinas, *Summa Theologiae*, I-II, 65,5. The text of the *Summa* used throughout the book is the Blackfriar's Edition, (New York: McGraw-Hill Book Co., 1963-1969).

3 Edouard Gagnon, *Les Vertus Théologales* (Montreal: Éditions de L'Institut Pie-XI, 1960), p. 277.

4 Aquinas, <u>ST</u>, II-II, 23,1. All references in this section are taken from this passage, q. 23 of the *Secunda Secundae*.

5 Servais Pinckaers, *Le Renouveau De La Morale* (Castermann, 1964), p. 89.

6 Guy DeBroglie, "Charité: Essai D'Une Synthèse Doctrinale," *Dictionnaire de Spiritualité* (1953), II, 676.

7 Aristotle, *Nichomachean Ethics*, trans. Martin Ostwald (Indianapolis:Bobbs-Merrill Publishing Co., 1962), 1155a2-5.

8 Aristotle, *Ethics*, 1170a10.

9 John M. Cooper, "Aristotle on Friendship," *Essays On Aristotle's Ethics*, ed. Amelie O. Rorty (Berkeley:University of California Press, 1980), p. 302.

10 *Ibid.*, p. 304.

11 *Ibid.*, pp. 308-317.

12 Aristotle, *Ethics*, 1156a10-25.

13 Cooper, "Friendship," p. 303.

14   Aristotle, *Ethics*, 1156a18.

15   Aristotle, *Ethics*, 1156b6-13.

16   Cooper, "Friendship," p. 308.

17   *Ibid*., p. 308.

18   Aristotle, *Ethics*, 1156b21-25.

19   Cooper, "Friendship," p.330.

20   Aristotle, *Ethics*, 1159b3.

21   Aristotle, *Ethics*, 1156b34-1157a1.

22   Aristotle, *Ethics*, 1097a15-1097b20.

23   Aristotle, *Ethics*, 1176b1-8.

24   Aristotle, *Ethics*, 1097b21-33.

25   Aristotle, *Ethics*, 1098a12-17.

26   Aristotle, *Ethics*, 1099a25-30.

27   Aristotle, *Ethics*, 1177a11-18.

28   Aristotle, *Ethics*, 1178b21-28.

29   Aristotle, *Ethics*, 1177b25-1178a3.

30   Avital Wohlman, "L'Élaboration des Éleménts Aristotéliciens dans la Doc-
     trine Thomiste de L'Amour," *Revue Thomiste*, LXXXII (1982), 249.

31   *Ibid*., pp. 251-252.

32   Richard Egenter, *Gottesfreundschaft. Die Lehre von der Gottesfreundschaft in
     der Scholastik und Mystik des 12. und 13. Jahrhunderts* (Augsburg: Dr. Benno
     Filser, 1928), p.43.

33   Aquinas, *ST*, II-II, 26,2.

34　Aquinas, *ST*, II-II, 25,12.

35　Aquinas, *ST*, I-II, 3,8.

36　Aquinas, *ST*, I-II, 2,8.

37　Aquinas, *ST*, II-II, 26,1. In this passage, Aquinas explicitly refers to God as the "principle of happiness." He writes: "Now we have already seen that charity loves God as the principle of eternal happiness, the sharing of which is the basis of this divine friendship between us. Consequently, among the objects that we love from charity, there must needs be some sort of order·with reference to God, who is the first principle of this love."

38　Paul Philippe, *Le Rôle De L'Amitié Dans La Vie Chrétienne Selon S. Thomas* (Rome: Angelicum, 1938), pp. 154-156.

39　Aquinas, *ST*, II-II, 24,2.

40　Aquinas, *ST*, I, 43,5.

41　Joseph Keller, "De Virtute Caritatis Ut Amicitia Quadam Divina," *Xenia Thomistica Theologica*, II (1925), 248.

42　Aquinas, *ST*, I, 38,2.

43　Aquinas, *ST*, I, 38,1.

44　Aquinas, *ST*, I-II, 106,1.

45　Aquinas, *Summa Contra Gentiles*, trans. Charles J. O'Neil (Garden City, New York: Hanover House, 1957), 4, c. 21, par. 8.

46　Aquinas, *De Caritate*, trans. Lottie H. Kendzierski (Milwaukee: Marquette University Press, 1960), a. 1.

47　Aquinas, *De Caritate*, a. 1.

48　Aquinas, *ST*, II-II, 23,2.

49　Aquinas, *De Caritate*, a. 1.

50　Aquinas, S̲T̲, I-II, 3,2.

51　Aquinas, S̲T̲, I-II, 3,5.

52 Aquinas, <u>ST</u>, I-II, 3,2.

53 R. Guindon, *Béatitude Et Théologie Morale Chez St. Thomas D'Aquin* (Ottawa: Éditions de l'Université d'Ottawa, 1956),p. 296.

54 *Ibid.*, p. 197.

55 Horvath, *Caritas*, p. 250.

56 Ilien, *Wesen*, p. 89.

57 *Ibid.*, p. 188.

58 Robert O. Johann, *The Meaning of Love* (Glen Rock, New Jersey: Paulist Press, 1966), p. 53.

59 *Ibid.*, p. 61.

60 *Ibid.*, p. 51.

61 *Ibid.*, p. 65.

62 *Ibid.*, p. 52.

63 E. Neveut, "La Vertu De Charité: Son Caractère Surnaturel," *Divus Thomas*, XL (1937), 145.

64 Aquinas, *ST*, I-II, 26,4.

65 Henri Noble, *L'Amitié Avec Dieu* (Paris: Desclée de Brouwer et Cie, 1932), p. 24.

66 Aquinas, *ST*, II-II, 27,2.

67 R.P. Adrien Pépin, *La Charité Envers Dieu* (Paris: Beauchesne, 1953), pp. 263-264.

68 Aristotle, *Ethics*, 1167a3-11.

69 Aristotle, *Ethics*, 1155b29-1156a5.

70 Johann, *The Meaning of Love*, pp. 46-47.

71 Philippe, *L'Amitié*, p. 29.

72   *Ibid.*, p. 30.

73   Aristotle, *Ethics*, 1157b18-25.

74   Aristotle, *Ethics*, 1158a5-10.

75   Aristotle, *Ethics* 1171b30-1172a7.

76   Aquinas, *Scriptum Super Sententiis Magistri Petri Lombardi* (Paris: P. Lethielleux, 1933), III, d.27, q.2,a.1.

77   Aquinas, *III Sent.*, d. 27, q.2, a. 1. "Illud autem quod ad alterum convivere facit, maxime amicitia est; quia, ut dicit Philosophus IX Eth., 'unusquisque conversatur cum amico suo in illis quae maxime diligit, et quae suam vitam reputat, quasi amico convivere volens.' Et ideo oportuit haberi quamdam amicitiam ad Deum, ut sibi conviveremus; et 'haec est caritas,' ut dictum est."

78   M. Coconnier, "Ce Qu'Est La Charité D'Après St. Thomas D'Aquin," *Revue Thomiste*, XIV (1906), 5-30.

79   Horvath, *Caritas*, p. 230.

80   Joseph Keller and Benoit Lavaud, "La Charité Comme Amitié D'Après S. Thomas," *Revue Thomiste*, XII (1929), 449.

81   Egenter, *Gottesfreundschaft*, p. 60.

82   Keller and Lavaud, "La Charité," p. 452.

83   Egenter, *Gottesfreundschaft*, pp. 42-43.

84   Conconnier, "La Charité," p. 13.

85   *Ibid.*, pp. 11-12.

86   Aquinas, *Summa Contra Gentiles*, trans. Vernon J. Bourke (Garden City, New York: Hanover House, 1956), 3, c. 19.

87   Keller, "De Virtute Caritatis," p. 256.

88   Henri Noble, "L'Amitié De La Charité," *La Vie Spirituelle*, XII (1925), 11.

89   Noble, *L'Amitié Avec Dieu*, pp,. 29-30.

90 Keller and Lavaud, "La Charité," pp. 452-453.

91 H.D. Simonin, "Autour De La Solution Thomiste Du Problème De L'Amour," *Archives d'Histoire Doctrinale et Littéraire du Moyen Âge*, VI (1931), 265-266.

92 Egenter, *Gottesfreundschaft*, p. 40.

93 Horvath, *Caritas*, p. 167.

94 Jean Mouroux, *The Christian Experience*, trans. George Lamb (New York: Sheed and Ward, 1954), pp. 263-264.

Chapter II

The Passions in the Service of Friendship with God

For Thomas, the virtues, though guided by reason, are not so much expressions of reason as expressions of something we love. That is why the virtues cannot be adequately appreciated apart from the passions. The purpose of a virtue is to help us attain and share in a good we seek, to unite us with what we love by forming us in its likeness. While reason certainly operates in directing us to the good of virtue, the passions and the affections are the stuff from which the virtues are formed. The task of the next two chapters is to demonstrate the tight connection in the *Prima Secundae* between the passions and the virtues; in fact, we will suggest that how Thomas understands the virtues and the function he gives them in the moral life cannot be grasped apart from the passions because it is precisely in terms of our sovereign love that the virtues make sense.

The passions have a critical role in the Thomistic moral economy, but exactly why they are so important cannot be discerned properly unless they are studied in light of the friendship with God all our love is meant to serve. Thomas's singlemost critical insight about the moral life is not just that everything we do is for the sake of something we love, but also that acting for the sake of what we love brings us likeness to what we love. However, if each of us is an expression of whatever we most love, then the successful outcome of the moral life depends on learning to love whatever can make us both happy and good.

This is why it is so important that charity be the sovereign love of our lives. Thomas calls us to be God's friends not only because God deserves our love, but also because if what we love has such inescapable significance on the person we become and the happiness possible to us, then our greatest passion has to be for God. As Thomas sees it, our love must take charity's form for any other love or any other passion would deny us the relationship necessary for happiness. Thus, for Thomas the key to moral wholeness lies not in circumventing the passions, but in cultivating a passion for God.

The formation of our sentiments according to that which is best for us is the most important concern of the moral life.[1] As chapter one established, what is best for us is to become a friend of God, and it is this friendship that the passions, principally love, should serve, and in terms of this friendship that their role in the Thomistic moral schema should be understood. If the passions are approached thusly, then not only will it be clear why love is the primary passion and the cornerstone of Thomas's moral theology, but it will also be clear why the love that guides and centers our life must be charity. In short, it is precisely this analysis of the passions that will illumine the importance of charity as the love which makes possible something as extraordinary as friendship with God. To show why this is so is the subject of chapter two.

A. The Passions Considered as Appetites

The most important thing to remember about the passions in the Thomistic moral schema is that the passions are the key to our moral perfection. What we love informs all we do, indeed so fully that eventually through our activity we are imbued with its likeness. Obviously, if the fullness of the moral life requires becoming a friend of God, and friends possess a similarity to each other that is so complete they are able to look upon each other as another self, then the Christian has to be passionate about God with a love called charity, for it is just that desire expressed through virtue that makes likeness to God possible. The genius in Thomas's account of the passions is fully disclosed when they are studied in view of friendship with God because when Thomas's analysis of the passions is applied to charity we glimpse how such a love renders us God's friends. In other words, Thomas claims charity makes us friends of God, but why it is just this love that achieves just this relationship can only be seen when charity is examined alongside Thomas's study of the passions. Charity is the love which perfects us because it makes us into the very thing that is our beatitude; however, why charity is perfecting and why it makes us God's friends is only understood when charity is considered not in itself, but as the most perfect form of the primary passion of love.

The most general term Aquinas uses to explain the affections or passions is appetite. He means by this the "order, ordination, and tendency of a potency toward its fulfillment, toward the object that will perfect it," and "in beings in which there is perception of attractive objects, there is a special penchant or tendency toward them, distinct from the intrinsic ordination of every potency of the being to its proper act. This tendency is an appetite, in the proper and formal sense of the term."[2] Aquinas describes the passions as appetites because he wants to underscore their active nature. As appetites, they seek or tend toward whatever attracts them as good because they see in those objects something they lack and need for their perfection and completion. It is the good perceived in the object that accounts for the attraction of the appetite.

Mouroux sees in Aquinas's description of the passions as appetites a picture of what it is to be human. It is not the case that only occasionally do men and women experience desires for certain goods because they see in them something necessary for their own completion. No, Mouroux argues, to be human is to be inclined continually and passionately to the goods we think will bring flourishing and fullness to our lives. In short, in Thomas's account of the passions as appetites there is an implicit anthropology. A human being is a creature of appetites, of powerful, perduring tendencies. A human being is one whose very nature is appetite, a tending toward the goods which allow the growth and perfection of the self.

Thus, as Mouroux explains, in Aquinas's pithy definition of an appetite as the tendency "of a potency toward its fulfillment," is a description of the most fundamental and constitutive activity of humans. As men and women, we are appetites, we are creatures of desire, because we are always, whether consciously or not, acting toward the goods we have chosen as our own. We are needy creatures hungry to possess all the things we think will bring us completeness. The whole of human life is an energy which strategically plots the achievement of what we have taken for our end. The most fundamental human movement is an appetite toward whatever a being sees as necessary for itself. Thus, the basic dynamism of the moral life is a longing for all the things we lack but love. It is this love for the array of goods which we take to comprise the development and completion of ourselves that is the most basic energy of the moral life. As Mouroux says,

> Man is a being in a state of desire....This appetite is his first, necessary, and unchanging movement....Until he reaches its end he is carried along by it irresistibly, in a great longing for infinity-he is open, desirous, hungry, needy....In man as a being proceeding towards his end, affectivity represents this fundamental, endlessly resurgent reaction towards the good, the 'proper', the end, or towards their opposites. Man is always thus in a state of tension or desire.[3]

In a similar passage, Richard Baker, in his excellent study, *The Thomistic Theory of the Passions and Their Influence Upon the Will*, graphically explains why to be human is to be a creature of powerful, driving desires:

> The existence of appetite in the world is surely a fact of ordinary experience. We are conscious within ourselves of a variety of inclinations and tendencies to objects which appear as suitable to us. In consequence of these inclinations, which we feel arising from within us, we are moved to act in some way to obtain those objects toward which we are inclined. The range of such objects is tremendous, embracing as it does at one extreme those things which satisfy our basic organic inclinations for food and sex, and at the other limit those things to which we are inclined by appetites for which we feel to be of a superior nature,-things such as beauty, truth, friendship, and virtue. By reason of these inclinations of all kinds, we are impelled to a constant activity to obtain their respective objects.[4]

It is important to note, however, that the passions are active only in a secondary sense. The activity does not commence with the appetite, but with the object towards which the appetite is attracted.

As we shall see, a passion properly describes the effect of the object upon a subject, whereas the appetite describes the response to whatever is loved or seen as good. Thus, the activity of the appetite begins not in itself, but in the attraction or appeal of whatever object is recognized as good. It is the perceived value of this object that acts upon the appetite and elicits its response.

This is morally significant for two reasons. First, it illustrates something is loved only because it is deemed necessary for a thing's perfection. We see something as good because we also see ourselves enhanced by possessing it. We love something and reach out toward it because we think it will contribute to our happiness. The fact that we have appetites, that we reach out and fervently strive for some things rather than others, reflects the lack of perfection suffered by each creature. Too, that our most fundamental and perduring tendency is exactly this reaching out and responding to something we lack and want to possess demonstrates our perfection resides not in ourselves, but precisely in this activity of striving for and being united to a good that can perfect us.

This parallels the argument stitched through chapter one that our perfection depends on a participation in a good that can give us a completion we can never give ourselves. For Thomas, the passions and affections, considered as appetites, are the linchpin of the moral life because it is through them that we are related to whatever is necessary for our perfection. Through the love we have for something, we not only move toward it, but are eventually joined to it. Viewed in one way, the passions describe the effect something we love has upon us. Viewed another way, the passions are appetites that reach out toward the things we love in order to possess them. From either perspective, Thomas's account of the passions and affections demonstrates that whatever is lacking to every human being is attained not from themselves, but only by their active participation in whatever perfects them. In a thoughtful passage, Richard Baker explains:

> To the mind of the philosopher, the constant movement which characterizes this world of 'ens mobile' is a sign of the initial lack of full perfection suffered by each creature. To achieve the fulness of being demanded by its nature,

each creature must act, so that by its acts it can obtain those things which it needs. The creature is given the perfection of existence and is endowed with various powers; but it must exercise these powers to secure from outside itself those things which can actualize its natural capacities. For this reason, "Everything both material and spiritual, has a relation to another; whence it is proper to everything to have an appetite...which is found in different beings in different forms" (*De Veritate*, q.23, a.1). It is through its appetites, therefore, that each creature is dynamically related to the things necessary for its full perfection. It is this "stretching out" to another that is called "appetitus" by the Scholastics.[5]

Secondly, that an appetite's activity is essentially a response to a good acting upon it is morally significant, especially in view of charity, because it indicates that the transformation of the person unto the good not only takes place in, but specifically is a relationship to that which perfects him. The effect of the loved object upon the appetite, and the appetite's response to what it experiences as good, constitutes a relationship, the activity of which perfects the appetite. It is not just that the object experienced as good contains that which the appetite lacks for its perfection, but more pointedly that such a good can only be acquired insofar as the appetite is continually related to its good both by reaching out towards it and being acted upon by it. Moral wholeness comes not through any activity, but expressly through the activity of being related to all that can make us good. As we shall see, it is within such a relationship that goodness, specifically virtue, is achieved because the openness of the subject to the good allows the subject to be formed in the good.

If it is true that our perfection depends on living in relationship to a good or set of goods that can perfect us, then what those goods are makes all the difference. We are creatures of love, creatures of tremendous desires that dominate our lives, that motivate us and in some way possess us, and if these desires are not to destroy us, they must be toward objects that are good. The good or goods to which we tend make us who we are-for Aquinas, we become what we love-and that is why we must, above all, learn to love God. If we think of this in view of friendship with God, then being in relationship with God through charity is exactly what is required if we are to achieve the fullness of our nature. Put differently, if what Thomas says about the appetites is right, then having something other than God as the constitutive, comprehensive relationship of our life will not only makes us something other than godly, but will also make it impossible for us to be either happy or good.

Thomas's analysis of the appetites supports this. He isolates three components in the appetitive movement that, taken as a whole, comprise a relationship: the subject of the appetite, the term toward which it tends, called the 'good' or the 'end', and the appetite itself, which constitutes what Geiger calls "un lien dynamique entre le sujet et son bien" which "révèle l'existence, entre le sujet et son bien, d'un rapport de complémentarité, fondé sur l'être même de l'un et de l'autre, et qui fait justement que l'un peut être le bien de l'autre pour autant qu'il en assure la perfection."[6] Geiger's comments underscore the moral import in how Thomas interprets the appetites because they indicate there is a constant tending of the appetite toward its term only because the term represents what the appetite is lacking for its completion. In this way, love, which names the tendency of the subject toward what will complete it, is prompted by a recognition of a subject's imperfection. The relationship established between the subject of the appetite and its term, precisely because that term is perceived as integral to the subject's completion, is love. As Thomas puts it, every appetite "is nothing more than a certain bent towards a thing that is wanted, a thing which is matching and complementary."[7]

Isolating these three elements again demonstrates that an appetite is not a sporadic, fortuitous tendency, but is, rather, a sustained, dynamic relationship between a subject and the object it loves. Moreover, the activity itself is the appetite's perfection because insofar as it is tending toward its good, it is receiving it and being formed in it. The relationship between the subject and the term is the appetite's perfection because it is that relational activity-Thomas calls it love-which allows the subject to participate in its good.

This analysis of the relationship between a subject and its good further illustrates the importance of charity as the fundamental love of our life. Charity is wholehearted passion for God, and it is the love which establishes the relationship with God that makes happiness and wholeness of life possible. As we saw before, happiness is a function of our most proper activity, and for Aquinas this is charity-friendship with God. What our analysis in chapter one showed is that our happiness depends on who we become, and who we become is a function of our love. Consequently, Thomas's analysis of the passions and affections as appetites suggests two things about the centrality of charity.

First, it shows that only charity sustains the relationship formative of one whose happiness will be God. Secondly, it demonstrates that for Thomas morality does not involve extirpating the passions, but transforming them. It is this transformation, which takes place through the charity-friendship we have for God, that ultimately enables us to be virtuous. In short, only those who delight in God can truly be good.

Moreover, being friends of God is possible only if we share God's form. This is key to understanding what makes the activity of charity integral to our eventual transformation in holiness. Thomas says the inclination or bent of an appetite comes from that appetite having a certain form.[8] An appetite is drawn toward a good the more it acquires its form; in short, the greater the sharing in its form, the greater the inclination towards it. In inanimate objects and animals, "natures and powers are innately inclined by God towards their proper ends and activities through the natural forms He has given."[9] These things instinctively tend towards their end. Their tendency is determined because the form which enables their perfection is not acquired, but inheres in them by nature.[10]

But it is not that way with us. We do not by nature possess the form that is our perfection, and when Thomas addresses this fact he makes an important distinction. First, since friendship with God is a supernatural end of which we are not by nature capable, the form or capacity which enables this relationship with God must be infused in us by grace. In the *Summa Contra Gentiles*, Thomas speaks of grace as the "supernatural form and perfection" which is "superadded to man whereby he may be ordered suitably to the aforesaid end,"[11] and in the *Summa*, he describes it as a form or power which is infused as a "kind of quality" inhering in the subject whereby he or she "may be moved by him [God] sweetly and promptly towards obtaining the eternal good."[12] Grace is "a certain habitual gift, by which spoiled human nature is healed, and once healed, is raised up to perform works which merit eternal life."[13] Thus, grace is the 'form' or 'nature' which enables friendship with God and makes the supernatural activity of charity possible. Grace achieves this by making us proportionate to our divine end, a proportion or fittingness we lack by nature.

On the other hand, what grace enables charity completes. Striking an analogy between nature and its operations, arguing that as a thing is so does it act, Aquinas says grace is the 'second nature' which precedes virtue and according to which the virtues operate. Grace imbues the soul "with a certain spiritual or Divine Being,"[14] a "kind of habitual state which is presupposed by the infused virtues, as their origin and root."[15] According to Aquinas, grace makes friendship with God possible (it is the 'root' or 'germ' of that friendship) but it does not achieve it. Grace enables friendship with God, but it is the virtue of charity which develops it. The intimacy with God that is our perfection is made possible through grace, but its fullness is the harvest of charity. Thus, resemblance to God is a function of both grace and charity inasmuch as grace is the 'gift' which is the necessary condition for the kind of activity displayed in charity. Grace makes possible the kinship with God that is our happiness, but charity achieves it. In this sense, the charity formed virtues are nothing more than grace expressed in activity, for they accomplish the end for which grace makes us capable. Grace operates mediately through the virtues, principally charity, for it is through the activity of the charity formed virtues that we participate in the divine goodness.

Therefore, in view of Thomas's remark that the appetite is inclined to the good insofar as it possesses the form of the good, this means our beatitude in God absolutely depends on the work of charity because it is only through the activity of that virtue that we increasingly acquire the form which enables us to grow in likeness to God. Grace makes the activity of charity possible, but only the friendship love of charity, continually undertaken as a way of life, opens us to be formed in the goodness of God. Thus, the greater and more steadfast our love for God, the more we take on the form of God; and the more we are formed in God, the greater is our inclination to God. Love is our perfection for it is the appetite, understood both as passion and as activity, through which we grow in the form of whatever perfects us. Consequently, if God is our perfection charity must be our love. Van Roey captures this well when he notes that if by grace we become children of God, our perfection is in becoming friends of God, and that is charity's work. Put differently, grace establishes one relationship between God and ourselves, but charity works for another. If by grace we are children of God, through charity we mature into the friends of God. Van Roey writes,

> Ex hac consideratione sequitur, responsum verum esse, at plane insufficiens, quo homo dicatur ad finem supernaturalem ordinari per gratiam sanctificantem. Verum est, inquam: nam per gratiam habitualem homo formaliter efficitur filius Dei adoptivus, ex Deo nascitur, semen divinum in se habet. Insufficiens tamen: quia ita nondum explicatur quomodo semen divinum in eo vivat et crescat ad plenitudinem vitae coelestis.[16]

B. The Primacy of Love in the Thomistic Account of the Passions

This analysis of the passions and affections as appetites helps us appreciate the primacy of love in Thomistic ethics. Simply put, if one's love is not right, everything else will be skewed. But exactly this also helps us see why the Christian's love must be charity. Thomas's treatment of the passions makes the primacy of charity all the more intelligible. The whole elaboration of Thomas's moral theology through the virtues and the Gifts presupposes a special love. In other words, the form the virtues must take if they are to give birth to the Gifts indicates why we must be right about our love. In the Thomistic schema of the moral life, everything hinges on the quality of one's love. The passions and affections are of utmost importance for Aquinas because the possibility of achieving beatitude and fullness of life balances on loving correctly from the start. Develop a love other than charity, and end up with a happiness other than God. Cultivate another kind of friendship, and become a different kind of person.

It is not by accident that Thomas begins the *Prima Secundae* asking about different kinds of happiness, whether our happiness be in money, fame, sensual pleasure, or anything other than God.[17] The reason he takes these various candidates for happiness so seriously is that he knows wherever we think our happiness is will determine what we love and how we love. Moreover, the quality of our love determines the quality of our actions, or the form the virtues take in us. From the perspective of Aquinas's analysis of the passions, how we start the moral life in love determines who we will be at the end. The kind of person we become is hardly accidental because our character is determined through our primary love. Thomas's study of the passions demonstrates that the moral life begins in love, is centered in love, and is guided by love. What is both frightening and promising about how Thomas positions love in the moral life is that the effect of what we love upon who we are is inescapable. If we set our heart on something we shall obtain it; in fact, we shall become it. For Aquinas, we become whatever we most love. It is this insight that explains why charity must be the love which rules our life and inspires all our actions.

When we appreciate the primacy Thomas gives to love, we begin to see that his picture of the moral life is really quite simple. Morality is a matter of desire, of powerful, relentless love. We seek what we love in everything we do. Love for some good motivates all our activity, it is the intention informing all we do. As Thomas says so well, "Now the good is always somewhat in the nature of an end or goal," and while the good is "last in actual achievement," it "comes first in one's intention." Thus, the moral life has three phases for Aquinas: first, there is the goal or end which the agent desires because he or she finds it attractive, "for nothing sets itself an end which it does not find in some way attractive or appropriate; second, it moves towards the goal; third, it comes to rest in the goal once it has been attained."[18]

For Aquinas, this is what the moral life involves: knowing what we love, moving toward it through action, and finally coming to possess it. Everything so precisely detailed in the *Prima Secundae* elaborates this fundamental insight that morality is most accurately portrayed as a love expressed through desire and brought to fullness in joy. If we love something we desire it, and desire seeks what we love through our actions. Finally, when through love we are brought to our good we are happy because it is only when we possess what we love that we are satisfied. As Thomas sees it, the moral life, indeed the formation of our character, begins with what we love and ends when we are one with it. That is why Gilson is right to say that understanding what morality involves must begin in a study of the passions, particularly the passion of love. As Gilson explains, for Aquinas everything turns on the quality of our love:

> When the moralist comes to discuss concrete cases, he comes up against the fundamental fact that man is a being moved by his passions. The study of the passions, therefore, must precede any discussion of moral problems, in which we will continually be encountering the passions as the matter, as it were, on which the virtues are exercised.[19]

What guides Aquinas's study of love is the simple insight that there is no love without something one loves. That is obvious, but it is also important because it demonstrates that the activity of love does not begin with the subject, but with the object that is loved. Yes, we irrepressibly love something, but we do not seek something to love as much as we discover something to love. As a passion, the activity of love does not commence with the subject; rather, love is a response to something felt to be good. It is the object perceived as valuable acting towards and upon the subject that prompts the response of love. When the good of the object is experienced, the agent reaches out to it, and thus a relationship of love is established; however, Thomas's point is that there is such a relationship only because there is a good which causes the agent's desire and begins the movement of love. Remember, Thomas explains, "that love is seated in the orectic faculty, and since that is a passive power, its object functions as the cause of its movement or action.

Therefore that which is the object of love will properly be called the 'cause' of love."[20]

Love is an appetite that tends towards whatever it finds desirable, but it does so only because it has first felt the object's attractive power. That Thomas sees the movement of love beginning not in the agent's creation of a good, but in her response to it is morally important because it suggests we do not create goodness, we respond to it. Thus, a crucial moral ability is discernment, the capacity to perceive what values are integral to wholeness. This may explain, for example, why Thomas sees the process of moral deliberation climaxing not in choice but consent.[21] As we shall see, for him moral perfection is not so much a question of freedom, but of surrender, of open-hearted vulnerability to the good that can perfect us.

And that is why we love. We love whatever we think will bring wholeness and completion to our life. Love is not the affection we have for any good, but is the passion expressly aroused by the good in which we believe our happiness consists. To say that we love whatever we think will perfect us is to recognize that our life really is co-extensive with the relationship we have with our primary good. This is why Leclercq says love governs life, and that the most important moral question is to know on what our heart is centered.[22] We have to know what we love because it is our desire for this good that stands behind all we do. In every action an intention for what we love is displayed.

It is this insight that allows Thomas to claim that charity is the formative principle of every activity for those who find their perfection in God. Love for whatever we take to be our supreme good informs all we do. More than that, the very nature of love is to work for our full assimilation in our good.[23] This is why Philippe calls love an activity of perfection. Love is our most basic and constant tendency toward the good, and since it expresses itself through all our activity, it is the means by which perfection is secured. Philippe explains:

Et c'est pourquoi l'amour humain est une tendance, une inclination vers cette perfection....En un mot, c'est l'amour qui est charge de procurer à l'être sa perfection, en l'inclinant vers elle comme vers son bien.[24]

Still, to say love is perfecting is not to say enough because we need to explain in more detail how this perfection takes place. Love perfects us not so much by movement toward the good, but by assimilation to the good. Of course, love signals movement insofar as it is a tendency, an active inclination toward what we desire, but what is perfecting about love is that through seeking what is good we are formed in what is good. Love is a perfecting activity because through it we take on the form of whatever good stands supreme for us. In other words, through love what we most desire becomes the form or identifying principle of all we do. Why? Because, Aquinas says, the form of every action is taken from the intention, goal, or end of the action.

Thomas says this at the beginning of the *Prima Secundae*, and it helps explain why love is so pivotal in his moral system. "Clearly all activities a power elicits," he writes, "come from it as shaped by its formal interest. And this, for the will, is being an end and a good."[25] Tucked so inconspicuously in the opening paragraphs of Thomas's account of beatitude, this passage offers an important clue for how he understands all moral activity, especially the virtues. Every act takes the form of its end. Every act is shaped by its formal interest in that each act is empowered by and formed in light of the end it seeks. For Thomas, human activity is always explicated best through the end to which the agent is most consistently attracted because it is the attractive power of that end that prompts human agency and gives it, as well as the agent, a special character. Every action is always in view of an end, and that is why all human activity is formed from and bears the quality of the good for the sake of which it is done. The form of any action comes from the end. As Thomas says, the specific character of any action "comes from the side of the object, which shapes the activity and determines the form it takes."[26] "Since the object of the will is being an end and good," he concludes, "it is clear that this is the determining principle of human acts as such....So then we may add that the end also provides moral acts with their proper specific character."27

But if the end we seek is the formal principle of all we do, love is perfecting because the good of the end is internal to the activity of love. Love perfects us in our good not, strictly speaking, by motion toward the good, but by assimilation to the good. The quality of the end is not something apart from us or outside us, but integral to love itself. Consequently, it is by love that we are made whole because through love we are formed in the good which perfects us. The identifying principle or form of all our behavior comes from whatever love centers and directs the will. It is this love that shapes the intention of all our behavior, forming not only what we do but who we become. For Aquinas the form of the action is also the form of the agent who acts because, as Paul Philippe argues, through our actions the quality of the act passes over into ourselves, qualifying and determining our character.28

Philippe's insight corresponds to our argument in chapter one that the perfection of men and women is an activity, but with the important qualification that such activity must be understood as a relationship of love. The agent is related to her or his end through love because the good of the end inheres in the activity itself as its constitutive form. Love relates us to our end precisely through the concept of form. That the form of the end is the form of the action explains how every act mediates to the agent the good she or he seeks. Therefore, because of the connection between agency and action, a connection forged because the principle of the end is internal to every action, every time one acts for the sake of an end, he or she is increasingly formed in and acquires the quality of that end. In short, love is perfecting because through activity the form of the end is mediated to the agent.29 The process is circular because the agent must act toward the end in order to acquire the character of the end, but it is in being thus determined by the goodness of the end that the agent is more readily inclined to seek it.

Applied to charity, Thomas's insight about the perfecting capacity of love takes on even greater meaning. Charity is a love that makes beatitude possible because the perfecting activity of charity is to form us in the goodness especial of God. Charity has to be the constitutive moral activity of all those whose end is God; but if it is it makes union with God possible because charity's love is formed in and according to the goodness of God. The principle of any action is taken from the end. If the end of charity's action is God, then the goodness of God becomes the form of the love that seeks God. And since the form internal to action comprises the bond between agency and action, the person whose acts bear charity's form takes on the goodness of God.

This parallels the argument of chapter one that happiness is not something extrinsic to virtue or even consequent to virtue, but the activity of virtue itself. It is important to allude to this now because it explains why the Christian's beatitude is the activity of charity-friendship with God. Charity is our beatitude because through this love we are sufficiently formed in the likeness of God to become the friends of God. Chapter one showed that for Thomas this friendship is our happiness. What we have learned now, however, is that such a claim can be sustained, and indeed make sense, only in light of Thomas's treatment of the formative influence of love on all human behavior. In short, without some appreciation of how Thomas understands both love and the relationship between what we do and who we become, one can hardly see why loving God ensures beatitude. But once we understand how Thomas sees the operation of love, then we can also understand that the connection he makes between charity and beatitude is not fortuitous; in fact, that charity-friendship with God is beatitude is entailed by Thomas's explication of love as the primary passion. Beatitude is inevitable for one whose love is charity because a friendship love for God unites us to God in the most radical, enduring way possible: it forms us in God's likeness. Once more we see that reading Thomas's treatise on the passions in light of charity-friendship not only underscores their significance, but also aids us in appreciating why charity is central to a moral schema whose purpose is to get us to God.

Nonetheless, the very fact that we are inclined to a good only inasmuch as we share its form indicates that the kinship or affinity we must feel for a good if we are to love it does not happen instantly, but is developed only as we continue to act toward a good. The sense that another thing is good for us, Thomas says, is not self-evident; rather, it is only when an affinity or connaturality with a good has been established through our suffering its form that we are able to love it as our good. Love demands "a sense of affinity with some good, the feeling of its attractiveness," and once that is attained it "produces the inclination to move towards the end in question."[30] The affinity we have towards an object is the cumulative effect of that object having acted upon us, shaping us in its form, so that the likeness we hence share with it causes us to be inclined towards it. In short, the affinity we feel for a good is not natural, but is developed in the measure that its formal goodness becomes our own.

But this means in order to love something we first have to suffer its effect. This means the affinity we have with something is not pre-established, but is wrought from that object acting upon us. The point is important for Aquinas because it demonstrates that affinity between the will and the object loved is possible only when the will has been turned toward that object, bent or inclined to it, by having suffered the attractive power of its good. We love something only when we have been changed by it. The affinity we have towards an object does not signify that our likeness to that object preceded our encounter with it, but that such likeness is a result of our having suffered its form. The affinity necessary for love requires the transformation of the will so that it is enough like the object loved to be inclined towards it.

Thus, Aquinas does not talk of us loving the genuinely good naturally or instinctively, for the will is indeterminate before any particular good; rather, he speaks of love as the "coaptatio appetitus." Love is possible only when a person has been in the presence of an object long enough to be changed by and according to that object's form. We love the truly good when our will has been adapted or fitted to it. In his *De Divinis Nominibus*, Thomas writes:

Ex hoc igitur aliquid dicitur amari, quod appetitus amantis se habet ad illud sicut ad suum bonum. Ipsa igitur habitudo vel coaptatio appetitus ad aliquid

velut ad suum bonum amor vocatur. Omne autem quod ordinatur ad aliquid
sicut ad suum bonum, habet quodammodo illud sibi praesens et unitum secundum quamdam similitudinem, saltem proportionis, sicut forma quodammodo est in materia inquantum habet aptitudinem et ordinem ad ip-
sam.[31]

Love has to be developed. The will must be gradually determined to the goodness of God. Patience and humility do the work
of love because love is possible only when we are willing to become
something we are not. This is what makes love difficult. Love is an
affection, a passion for that which perfects us, but love is elicited
habitually-it is truly second nature to us-only when we have suffered or taken on the form of the object loved. Of course natural
loves remain. The hungry man still naturally loves food, the cold
man warmth. But Aquinas has in mind a love which makes for
virtue, a love which perfects us by enabling our happiness. And the
love necessary for happiness is not natural to us, but is developed
only as our wills are conformed to the goodness of God. Put simply,
we only know we are to love God when we have already become
enough like God to love God.

This is why Gilson's comment that "love is this first onset felt by
the soul at the touch of an object which it knows to be intimately
allied to it,"[32] has to be qualified. Aquinas would respond that insofar as moral goods are concerned, we do not know we are
"intimately allied" to whatever is best for us prior to risking being
changed by it. The intimacy required by love does not arise naturally, but is the consequence of being painstakingly transformed by
the object's goodness. What Gilson describes is not exactly love, at
least in the moral sense. It may be desire. It may be concupiscence.
But to be a love whose activity is our perfection, the attraction we
have toward that object must be fashioned by it creating a similarity
between us and itself. Gilson is closer to Aquinas when he says love
"is a modification of the human appetite by some desirable object"
made known "in the fact that the appetite takes pleasure in this
object," but Aquinas, when considering love from a moral perspective, would not agree that "such pleasure or complacency is, so to
speak, an immediate experiencing of natural affinity, of the fact

that the living being and the object it is meeting are somehow complementary."[33] For Aquinas, love requires a history with a good. Love describes an attraction to a good, but that is the result of time spent in its presence, of a relationship sustained long enough for the good to act upon the subject and an affinity or kinship to emerge. Ilien sees this better than Gilson. Like Gilson, he calls love a "tendency" or "inclination" towards an end, but sees this as a function of an "aptitude" or "proportion" established between the subject and its good:

> Nun setzt eine Tendenz zu einem Ziel für Thomas eine gewisse "aptitudo sive proportio ad finem" voraus, ein Prinzip, das noch eingehend zu behandeln sein wird. Diese "aptitudo sive proportio", die das wesentlich tendenzielle appetitive "Hin" des Subjekts zu dem als Finis erstrebten Objekt begründet, nennt Thomas "amor", der (unter psychologischem Aspekt) als "complacentia boni", als erstes Gefallen-gefunden-Haben am Objekt, zur auslösenden Bewegung innerhalb der konkupiszüblen Passionen und damit zum Grundphänomen des gesamten affektiven Bereichs wird.[34]

If we consider what Thomas says about the conditions for love in light of charity, we realize the only way it will ever appear to us that we should love God more than anything else is if we first let our will be formed by God. To love God we have to suffer the goodness of God. To be turned to God in all things and to seek God in friendship, our hearts have to be refined by the fire of God's love acting upon us. To love someone is to suffer their form, to be vulnerable to precisely what accounts for their goodness, and, as Horvath says, by this Thomas means loving God begins not in any inclination we have to God, but by our willingness to have our love transformed so we become enough like God to love God. It is just this inclination developed in us by the love and goodness of God that enables us to love God as friend. To have charity, our love has to be transformed both in and according to the love of God. "Die Liebe ist also einer wohlgefallende Hinneigung auf Grund der Anpassung der Affekte," Horvath writes. "Nach dieser langer Erklärung fassen wir also mit Thomas das Wesen der Liebe so zusammen: Die Liebe bedeutet eine wohlgefallende

Umwandlung des Affektes in die geliebte Person."[35]   Similarly, Egenter says for Thomas

> die Liebe bedeutet eine Transformation des liebenden Affektes in die geliebte Sache. Diese Transformatio besagt ein Bestimmtwerden und Zur-Ruhe-Kommen des Affektes, wodurch dieser in den zustand der complacentia, des Wohlgefallens an dem geliebten Gegenstand versetzt wird, der gleichbedeutend erscheint mit einer inneren Zuneigung zu dem Geliebten.[36]

This look at Thomas's analysis of the primacy of love helps us see why his treatise on the passions is best interpreted in light of charity-friendship with God. In chapter one we said that for Thomas the moral life is charity-friendship with God both in its most proper activity and its ever intended goal. But charity is love, a very special, distinctive love, that joins us in friendship with God, a love whose perfection is the happiness of counting God another self. What this examination of love has shown us is that the relationship we need with God if we are to be transfigured in the very holiness of God and be happy as God is happy, is possible only if we first allow ourselves to be loved, only if we first are open to suffering the goodness of God. Charity is friendship love for God, and what Thomas's study of love has suggested is that we can only be friends of God when we first submit to the love by which we can love. Loving God begins not in our activity, but in our willingness to let ourselves be loved. Love is an activity, but it is active only in response to a good that makes it the activity it is.

This is what Thomas's study of the passions tells us about our ability to love. It seems a simple insight, but it is significant because it will give us a very different, probably surprising, reading of the virtues. It will also clarify why the virtues are not separable from the Gifts, but reach their perfection in them. If we understand what Thomas says about love, and think of it in terms of charity, we will see not only why charity has to be the heart of his moral system, but also why every virtue is related to charity both as its source and as the love every virtue serves. To understand how Aquinas's explication of love qualifies our sense of the virtues, especially why the virtues perfect us, in the final section of this chapter we must consider more fully how important it was for Thomas to call love a passion, and precisely why this rendering of love enables our perfection unto God.

C. Being Perfected by the God We Love

Aquinas's moral theology argues elegantly that we are not yet who we should be and we do not have within ourselves whatever is lacking for our perfection. This is why when Thomas first speaks of love, he considers it a passion. "Now passion or passivity," Thomas writes, "implies by its very nature some sort of deficiency: a thing is passive in so far as it is in potentiality to being actualized and thus improved. Those creatures therefore that come nearest to God, the first and completely perfect being, have little of potentiality and passivity in them; others, of course, have more." Thomas's point is that "an excellence obviously increases as the first and unique source of the excellence is approached," while a "deficiency increases, however, not with proximity to, but with distance from, what is perfect and supreme: that is precisely what makes a thing defective."[37]

This is probably the most pithy summary of Aquinas's moral theology: the quality of our moral life is directly proportionate to our nearness to God. The nearer to God we are the better we are because God is the excellence by which we are made good. This also explains why love is a passion. A passion signifies something is perfected the more it receives from and is drawn closer to whatever can perfect it. But it cannot perfect itself because the form for its perfection comes not from itself, but from outside itself.

For Thomas, passion signifies not only that something is lacking to a thing's perfection, but also that by itself it is unable to provide what it most needs. It is not only deficient, it is inherently deficient because it cannot supply for itself, but must receive, that by which its excellence is achieved. Passion suggests openness, the capacity to take on what is lacking in one's perfection, and to call love a passion means our perfection comes principally not from our activity, but from our openness to God, our willingness to be vulnerable to God, and our desire to be absorbed into God.

If "an excellence obviously increases as the first and unique source of the excellence is approached," then the plot of the Christian moral life is to enable us to absorb God. As a passion, any love is essentially openness, and charity is essentially openness for God. This does not mean charity is no virtue, but as a virtue its express activity is to open us further to God. And if "a thing is passive in so far as it is in potentiality to being actualized and thus improved," in charity we are improved only insofar as our activity renders us more supple to God. Charity is the love that acknowledges we become more like God to the degree that we are willing to be open to God. As a virtue charity is essentially openness, the activity that makes us vulnerable to the God by whom we are.

Aquinas considers the moral life from a very different perspective. True, his is an ethics of virtue, but to say the virtues must be formed in charity suggests the strategy of every virtue is not simply to perform a certain action, but through that action to allow the agent to receive and inhere more deeply in the quality which perfects him. Each virtue is fueled by love, and that means each virtue is a passion, an ongoing and ever deepening openness for the God by whose presence we are. There is a paradox woven through Thomas's account of the virtues that is revealed when their connection to the passions is acknowledged, and it is this: through the activity of every virtue we avail ourselves to be acted upon by God. That is why the virtues perfect us. They perfect us not simply through our own activity, but because through activity informed by charity we become ever more vulnerable to the perfection of God. The virtues strengthen us by making us defenseless before God's love. And lest this sound far-fetched, consider how Thomas describes a passion:

> The Latin verb 'pati', to suffer or undergo or be acted upon, is used in three ways. First, in a perfectly general sense, it is used whenever any quality is received, even if the recipient loses nothing in the process....However, this would be better styled 'acquiring' a new quality than 'suffering' something. More strictly, the word 'pati' is used when a thing acquires one quality by los-

ing another; and this may happen in two ways. Sometimes the quality lost is one whose presence was inappropriate in the subject: for example, when an animal is healed, it may be said to undergo healing, for it recovers its health by shedding its illness. At other times, the opposite happens: for example, a sick man is called a 'patient' because he contracts some illness by losing his health.[38]

Does this mean the moral life is essentially a healing? Is charity the virtue by which we are made whole by acquiring the goodness which restores us to health? Yes. This is madness to anyone schooled to think the virtues are those activities by which we perfect ourselves, but it is a reading of the virtues which is inescapable once we perceive their connection to love and know what it means to call love a passion. This does not deny the virtues perfect us; they just do not perfect us the way we usually think. They perfect us only because through the virtues we rid ourselves of one quality in order to receive from God another. This is what happens when the virtues are linked to the passions. The virtues become those activities by which we ready ourselves to be acted upon by God. Through charity we are healed because a friend of God is one most willing "to suffer or undergo or be acted upon" by God. Through charity we are healed because being a friend of God means we have lost all those qualities which made us strangers to God in order to be formed by God into God's friends. As Gilson says, a passion

is an activity which consists in the soul's undergoing something. Now to undergo or suffer, in the broadest sense, means simply to receive; but in the most precise sense, it means essentially to bear; that is to say, to receive an action which must imply a certain suffering and loss.[39]

As articulating a passion for God, any virtue formed in charity is a particularly fitting way we "undergo God," a particularly fitting way we suffer the form of God or bear the goodness of God. Genuine virtue begins not in activity but receptivity. In order for the Christian to be good, she or he must first be receptive to the love that makes them good.

By prefacing his analysis of the virtues with an account of the passions, Aquinas makes an important point for how the virtues are to be understood. The link Aquinas forges between the passions and the virtues signifies that we can only be virtuous when we have first been formed by the love of God. As Leclercq puts it, "Passion vient de *pati*, souffrir; la passion est donc passive, c'est-à-dire qu'elle naît sous une influence extérieure; elle est effet de l'action de l'agent dans le patient."[40] The same is true of the virtues. They are 'born under the influence' of our sovereign love because they are formed by our most abiding passion. In order to be truly virtuous, we must be passionate about God. As Henri Noble says, we must be "passif sous la domination" of God, and this means we are not only vulnerable to God, but vulnerable in the deepest way possible: God is the One by whom we are.[41]

Furthermore, by arguing that each virtue is formed by the love from which it proceeds, Thomas implies that what a virtue needs for its perfection is not something it gives itself, but something it receives by being formed in the goodness of its end. This is also why the virtues are best understood as strategies of love. Virtues only exist when there is a love that prompts them, a love by which they are active. Virtues are activities formed from love, but in order for any act to be truly a virtue, it must first have suffered or taken on the goodness of its end.

Applied to charity, we can only act towards God as friends when we have first opened ourselves to God and allowed ourselves to suffer the goodness of God. Linking the passions to the virtues means our virtues can be rightly formed only when our love has first been transformed; therefore, we cannot presume to be virtuous-we are not friends of God-unless we have been changed by the good from which we can rightly love. In other words, what a charity-centered moral theology shows us is that our virtue begins not with ourselves, but with God.

We have to become like God in order to act towards God, and that likeness is attained through love, expressly charity. Thomas espouses a charity-centered moral theology because he knows love is the most formative activity of which we are capable. Our love makes us who we are because in loving a person what we receive from them is not just any quality, but the form which most distinctly makes them who they are. Love is a passion, and like any passion it means we acquire something we did not have before. But what distinguishes the passion of love is that what is acquired through love is the form of the loved one. This is what Henri Noble says in his study of the passions in the moral life: "En un sens plus déterminé,-proprie dit saint Thomas,-'passio' désigne non plus réceptivité quelconque dans un sujet, mais, dans ce même sujet, réception d'une forme qui provoque la perte d'une forme contraire."[42]   In charity the form of God replaces whatever in us is not of God. For Thomas, what is morally striking about love is that love is the passion whereby one form is replaced by another.

That is why we become whatever we love. When we receive the form of something we acquire exactly the quality which makes it one thing rather than another. Form is the "shaping principle within an object,"[43] that by which something is most precisely constituted. In *De Virtutibus*, Thomas writes: "A thing is distinguished in its species by what is formal to it. Now in each thing the formal element is what completes its definition. For it is the ultimate difference which constitutes the species as such, so that by this differentia a thing differs specifically from other things."[44] Or as R.M. Schultes, in his excellent article, "De Caritate Ut Forma Virtutum," says: "Forma in rebus naturalibus dicitur id quod rei dat speciem, perfectionem, principia operativa quibus sc. res operatur."[45]

That is why it is so important to love rightly. What we love makes us. What we love forms us in the being of the one we love. We are transformed by whatever we love because through love we lose the form we had possessed in order to take on another. Love is being possessed by whatever we love, and Thomas means this as radically as possible because through love the form of the beloved enters into us and makes us something new. There is no greater vulnerability than love because in love we are defined not through ourselves, but through whatever we love. For instance, through charity we are able to see God as another self because in that love God determines who we are. Thomas refuses to stop short of a total making over of our life by God. The form of God is what makes God God, that, as Schultes says, which gives God "speciem, perfectionem, principia operativa quibus sc. res operantur," and it is that form we receive in charity. Charity is the love through which we are depossessed of all that is not God in order to be possessed by God. The fullness of the moral life for Thomas is this full possession of ourselves by God, and it is not too much to say that for Thomas in charity it is God who gives the species, perfection, and operative principle of our life.

To love God is to be conformed to the ways of God. We have always known that. But Thomas pushes us to see it as deeply as possible. We are conformed to God from within, from our deepest being. Through charity we come to resemble God. We are good because we have taken on the character of God. That sounds extreme, but that is what Aquinas means by the love of charity: we are friends of God because we have suffered the form of God.

There is something incredibly beautiful, but also astonishing and maybe even unnerving in what Aquinas says of love because to love God in charity means we lose control over our life at precisely that point where the risk is greatest: we lose control over our self. It is one thing to receive from another qualities which might change us, but do not really touch what it means for us to be a self. With charity it is different. To love God in charity is to give God that unnerving control of being able to determine ourself, and that is to love absolutely because it means the form we are willing to lose in charity is exactly that sense of self and identity we most cherish. Charity is that death to self, that mysterious, unsettling denial to which the Gospel calls us because it means we suffer the loss of one kind of self and trust in the one formed in us by God.

That sounds drastic, but it is the change risked in charity. In the *Scriptum Super Sententiis*, Thomas says in love the lover is transformed in the interior of the one loved ("cum amans in interiora amati transformatur"), so that the God we love enters into us and remakes us from within, purifying, cutting away, and wholly transforming us according to the divine goodness. Aquinas continues: "Alia est unio quae facit unum simpliciter, sicut unio continuorum et formae et materiae; et talis est unio amoris, quia amor facit amatum esse formam amantis...."[46] In love, the one who loves is made according to the form of the one who is loved, and Thomas says this is what happens in our charity-friendship with God. The love of charity transforms us according to God. God becomes the norm or rule of our life because in charity it is God who enters into us, God whom our love absorbs, and therefore, God who forms and transfigures us according to Himself.

This is how the transformation of the affections necessary to be a friend of God occurs. Our love is changed not directly by our own efforts, but by our willingness to be imbued by the form of the one we love. Our affections are purified by an ascesis, but the very special ascesis of being open to and suffering the goodness of God. It is like the relation between matter and form because as matter is changed and shaped according to its form, so are we by receiving the form of the beloved. It does not mean, as Horvath explains, that in loving God we become God, but it does mean that in loving God we are filled and transformed according to God, and thus become, if not identical to God, similar to God:

> Der Liebende 'imbuitur omnino' durch die Form der geliebten Sache, d.h. der Liebende wird durch die Form des geliebten Gegenstandes erfüllt und verändert, wie die Materie durch die Form....Damit will Thomas natürlich keine physische Einheit der Liebenden behaupten. Das ist unmöglich, sie haben beide schon die Formen und bleiben immer zwei Seiende. Der Sinn dieser Anwendung des Begriffs Materie und Form auf die Liebe ist nichts anderes, als die Betonung der Transformatio, die Umwandlung der Affekte des Liebenden in den Geliebten. Wie die Materie durch die Form ganz verändert und durchgeformt wird, so wird auch der Liebende durch die Liebe verändert.[47]

Our affections are transformed by receiving the form of the loved one. We love rightly, Horvath suggests, to the degree we allow ourselves to be determined by God. In short, with charity we become God's friend because through charity we are so impressed with the form of God that God's very goodness becomes our own. Thus, because we have received God, we are increasingly inclined to God. Horvath explains:

> Der Geliebte ist in den Liebenden eingeprägt. Durch diese Einprägung wird der Geliebte zuerst dem Liebenden wohlgefallen, ihm angenehm

(connaturalis) sein und der Liebende neigt sich zu dem Geliebten....Die neue Übereinstimmung, die vom Geliebten kommt, entspricht der früheren Formähnlichkeit und macht den Geliebten für den Liebenden angenehm.[48]

Love is a perfecting activity, but only because its express activity is receptivity to the form of what will perfect us. Love is a perfecting activity, but perhaps not in the way we usually think. For Thomas, the receptivity of love is vulnerability to the good which is loved. And Thomas means this literally. In charity we are so receptive to God that we risk being wounded by God. To love God is to seek this woundedness because that vulnerability, unflinching and extreme, is a measure of how much we desire God. Friends of God, at least the saints, seek being wounded by God because it is only through God, and not themselves, that they can love God as they ought. Thomas twists the logic of love by suggesting the perfection of love comes not when we possess the thing we love, but when we are possessed by it; it is then that God can enter into us and perfect us.

Again this underscores the importance of Thomas describing love as a 'passive power'. His point is not to deny that as a virtue charity is an activity, but to insist it is essentially an activity of openness; in fact, Thomas argues it must be this activity of openness because we are not perfected directly by ourselves, but only insofar that through our activities we receive more fully the form of the God who perfects us. For Aquinas charity is a virtue of vulnerability, a virtue of abiding, extreme openness to God, because it is by receiving the form of God that we grow into God's friends. This insight can be traced back to Aquinas's earliest writings. In the *Scriptum Super Sententiis*, Aquinas says an appetite is perfected according to the form of its good, and that it is satisfied or at rest only when it is finally joined to its good:

Dicendum quod amor ad appetitum pertinet. Appetitus autem est virtus passiva....Omne autem passivum perficitur secundum quod formatur per formam sui activi et in hoc motus ejus terminatur et quiescit.... Similiter quando affectus vel appetitus omnino imbuitur forma boni quod est sibi objectum, complacet sibi in illo et adhaeret ei quasi fixum in ipso; et tunc dicitur amare ipsum. Unde "amor nihil aliud est quam quaedam transformatio affectus in rem amatam."[49]

In his classic article, "Autour De La Solution Thomiste Du Problème De L'Amour," H.D. Simonin offers a helpful explanation of this passage:

> La raisonnement trouve son point de départ dans le caractère passif de l'appétit. Or, tout être passif reçoit sa perfection et sa forme de l'agent qui lui correspond. La possession de cette forme met un terme à son mouvement et lui procure un état de repos. Tel est le cas de l'intelligence qui reçoit la perfection qui lui est propre de la possession de la forme intelligible. Tel est aussi le cas de l'appetit, lorsqu'il possède la forme du bien qui est son objet. Il s'y complaît, il y adhère fixement, on dit alors qu'il l'aime. Ainsi l'amour est-il essentiellement la transformation de l'affectivité en la chose aimée....[50]

As Simonin notes, in his earliest writings Aquinas focused on the passivity of love, emphasizing that to love means we receive our form from the object we love, and that our perfection increases the more deeply that form determines us. Aquinas in no way denies the activity of love, but gives it a specific interpretation. Since love signals a deficiency and what is loved contains whatever the lover lacks, love's interest is to receive and be completed by the form of the beloved. And as Ilien adds, when Thomas speaks of the activity of love as a 'taking on' of the form of the beloved, he also implies that in some sense the lover loses his or her own form in order to suffer the form of the beloved and be one with it:

> Die Liebe als entitatives Besitzergreifen der Forma des Geliebten bedeutet die Vollendung der appetitiven Bewegung und damit das letzte Ziel der gesamten affektiven Aktivitaten....So ist aus der Tatsache, dass der Amor den Besitz der "forma" des Geliebten durch den Liebenden besagt, das Einswerden beider zu begrunden, wodurch die dionysische Formel von der Liebe als "vis unitiva et concretiva" bestatigt wird. Durch die Ubernahme der Forma des Geliebten verliert der Liebende gewissermassen die eigene Forma und "erleidet" das Ausser-sich-Sein. So ist die Unio der Liebenden eine absolute und die hochstmogliche Form von Unio uberhaupt, vergleichbar derjenigen von Materie und Form.[51]

This taking on the form of the beloved is what enables friendship. Remember that friends are those who are so much like each other that they consider each other another self. But to behold each other that way means the similarity is precisely a similarity in form, a sharing in that which makes each of the friends a self. And yet, what makes this so striking is that friends are not those who share two different forms, not even those who share each other's form; rather, friends behold each other as 'another self' exactly because they share the same form, because the self of each is formed from the good which binds the friends and constitutes their friendship. That is why the unity possible in friendship is so extreme. In short, in friendship we really can behold the other as another self because the good which bonds the friendship is the determinative principle for the self of our friend as well as our own. In question twenty-seven of the *Prima Secundae*, this is what Thomas says:

> The first of these two kinds of similarity (similarity in which two things actually possess the same qualities) gives rise to love-of-friendship or love-of-goodwill, for the fact that two people are alike in having some form means that they are in a sense, one in that form....The result is that the affections of the one are bent upon the other as being one with himself, and he wishes well to the other as to himself.[52]

As Keller and Lavaud add, Aquinas argues that resemblance is the cause of love, but what makes two people resemble each other in the particular love of friendship is that friends share the same form.[53] That is why we are able to wish for the friend's good we do our own. The friend is one with us. Our good is the same. And our self lives in and through the self of the friend because by sharing one form with them, exactly the good which makes them who they are also makes us ourself. Pépin rightly says "l'homme est spontanément parté à aimer quelqu'un dans la mesure où celui-ci lui ressemble, comme ayant même 'forme'...."[54] One reason we love our friends is because insofar as they are, we are. We love them because in loving them we share more deeply the good which forms us both.

Think about what this means when our friendship is with God. There is a way charity-friendship is different. With charity, the form that shapes the friendship is not something external to the friends, but is the goodness of God. God is the form of charity-friendship because God's goodness is the measure of the kind of person we must become if we are to share God's joy. Egenter claims that what is true of friendship love generally is also true of the charity-friendship we have with God. "Der Gottesfreundschaft müss, wie jeder Freundschaft,"he writes, "eine unio similitudinis zugrunde liegen. Diese 'unio similitudinis' bedeutet eine ähnlichkeit der Form...."[55]

That is correct, but only if we add that the similarity in form which is proper to charity is achieved only insofar as we acquire the goodness of God. The friendship we have with God turns on sharing the form of God. Friendship with God demands coming to resemble God, being as much like God as possible, and there is no greater likeness than a likeness in form. We attain the status of friendship with God to the degree we are able to take on the form of God, and in that is our perfection.[56]

But it also means, as we discussed in chapter one, that not only is our proper self being a friend of God, but more pointedly, that we can be a self only insofar as we are God's friend. A thing is perfected by receiving the form of whatever it lacks for its perfection. Applied to friendship, this means we are perfected by receiving the form of the good we share with our friend. Applied to God, it means our perfection is God and we are more fully a self in the measure that God's form becomes our own. Thus, charity suggests that we are a self only when we allow ourselves to be formed by God; that is, we are a self only in friendship with God not just because our life has its meaning in relation to God, but more exactly because it is in receiving the 'other self' who is God that our own self is bestowed. That is why Keller says we are able to look upon God as 'another self', as a self who is one with us. That is why we are able to love God as ourself and desire God's good as we do our own, not because God's self is identical to our own, but because it is from God and according to God that our self is formed.[57]

This point is crucial for understanding the ongoing argument of this book, especially our contention that the moral life for Aquinas is a life of friendship with God culminating in the perfect friendship of the Spirit. For now, however, it is sufficient to see why we can love God as friend in the measure we bear God's form, and why such ongoing perfection is the work of charity.

We should love God as much as possible. That is the ongoing chorus of Thomas's moral theology. And what this chapter has indicated is why this is not just an expression of Thomas's piety, but an absolute moral necessity. We should love God as much as possible first because it is that passionate desire for God which enables us finally to love as God loves, and secondly because if our love determines who we are, when we love God we become like God. What Thomas pleads for us to see in the *Prima Secundae* is that everything depends on what we finally love. We cannot afford to love carelessly. It is tragic to love wrongly. As Thomas reminded us, people who love wrongly are neither happy nor good. The argument of this chapter has been that everything is an expression of what we love. Each of the emotions turns on the quality of our love. The virtues are activities by which we not only possess what we love, but also are formed according to it. That is why we become the very thing we love: the object of our affections enters into us and ultimately possesses us. Our self is mediated through what we love. We take on its likeness. We image its character. And someday we are even one with it.

Thomas studied theology because he loved God. And all of his moral theology in the *Summa* is the impassioned plea of a man who delighted in God as friend, for us also to risk friendship with God that we might know, as Thomas did, the joy and peace only charity can give. The *Prima Secundae* is a hymn to those resplendent in the likeness of God. But it is a hymn of great verve, a hymn of thunderous conviction, because Thomas does not want us to be trapped in a love that would cost us the happiness of God.

At the beginning of this chapter we said interpreting Thomas's account of the passions in light of charity would not only focus the strategy behind Thomas's explication of them, but would also illumine why Thomas had to have a charity-centered moral theology. The point of the *Prima Secundae* is to show us we have to love God in order to be happy, and Thomas's account of the passions explains why. It is through love that we are united with what makes us happy because as a passion love is the activity by which we are opened to what will perfect us. Correspondingly, charity is the activity of beatitude because it is the love which transfigures us into the goodness of God, thus making us God's friends, and the love which sustains this relationship, this colloquy of love, unto ever deepening beatitude.

The argument of this book is that the moral schema of the *Prima Secundae* is best understood if Thomas's account of the passions, the virtues, and the Gifts of the Spirit is not only read in light of charity-friendship, but also seen in its service. If this is done, not only will what Thomas says about the passions, the virtues, and the Gifts be clearer, but they, in turn, will render more convincingly why being friends of God is absolutely essential to Thomas's conception of the Christian moral life. Simply put, to love something more than God is to lose the happiness of God.

Still, as we said in chapter one, happiness is an activity of virtue. How our sense of the virtues changes when we consider them not only in terms of charity, but also in connection with the passions has already been hinted in this chapter. In chapter three we shall examine this more fully, asking not only why we need the virtues to become a friend of God, but especially how the virtues change when the good they serve and the purpose they are to achieve is charity-friendship with God.

Notes

1 Jacques Leclercq, *Les Grandes Lignes de la Philosophie Morale* (Louvain: Publications Universitaires de Louvain, 1954), p. 357.

2 Joseph Buckley, *Man's Last End* (Saint Louis: B. Herder Book Co., 1949), p. 127.

3 Mouroux, *The Christian Experience*, p. 237.

4 Richard Baker, *The Thomistic Theory of the Passions and Their Influence Upon the Will* (Ann Arbor: Edwards Brothers, Inc., 1941), p. 1.

5 *Ibid.*, p. 3.

6 Louis Geiger, *Le Problème de L'Amour Chez St. Thomas d'Aquin* (Montreal: Institute d'Etudes Medievales, 1952), pp. 41-42.

7 Aquinas, *ST*, I-II, 8,1.

8 Aquinas, *ST*, I-II, 8,1.

9 William R. O'Connor, *The Eternal Quest* (New York: Longman, Green and Co., 1947), p. 116.

10 *Ibid.*, p. 110.

11 Aquinas, *Contra Gentiles*, 3, c. 150.

12 Aquinas, *ST*, I-II, 110,2.

13 Aquinas, *ST*, I-II, 109,9.

14 Aquinas, *De Virtutibus*, trans. John Patrick Reid (Providence, Rhode Island: The Providence College Press, 1951), a. 10.

15 Aquinas, *ST*, I-II, 110,3.

16 J.E. Van Roey, "De Charitate Forma Virtutum," *Ephemerides Theologicae Louvaniensis*, I (1924), 47.

17 Aquinas, *ST*, I-II, 2,1-6.

18 Aquinas, *ST*, I-II, 25,2.

19 Etienne Gilson, *The Christian Philosophy of St. Thomas Aquinas*, trans. L.K. Shook (New York: Random House, 1956), p. 271.

20 Aquinas, *ST*, I-II, 27,1.

21 Aquinas, *ST*, I-II, 15,1,4.

22 Leclercq, *Les Grandes Lignes*, p. 427.

23 Paul Philippe, *L'Amitié*, p. 7.

24 *Ibid.*, p. 7.

25 Aquinas, *ST*, I-II, 1,1.

26 Aquinas, *ST*, I-II, 9,1.

27 Aquinas, *ST*, I-II, 1,3.

28 Philippe, *L'Amitié*, p. 7.

29 *Ibid.*, p. 4.

30 Aquinas, *ST*, I-II, 26,1.

31 Aquinas, *De Divinis Nominibus* (Rome: Marietti, 1950), c. 4,1.

32 Etienne Gilson, *Moral Values and the Moral Life*, trans. Leo Richard Ward (Saint Louis: B. Herder Book Co., 1931), p. 106.

33 Gilson, *The Christian Philosophy*, p. 272.

34 Ilien, *Wesen*, p. 95.

35 Horvath, *Caritas*, pp. 161-162.

36 Egenter, *Gottesfreundschaft*, p. 15.

37   Aquinas, *ST*, I-II, 22,2.

38   Aquinas, *ST*, I-II, 22,1.

39   Gilson, *Moral Values*, pp. 91-92.

40   Jacques Leclercq, *La Philosophie Morale De Saint Thomas Devant La Pensée Contemporaine* (Louvain: Publications Universitaires de Louvain, 1955), p. 295.

41   Henri Noble, *Les Passions Dans La Vie Morale* (Paris: P. Lethielleux, 1931), I, 17.

42   *Ibid.*, p. 18.

43   Thomas Gilby, Appendix, *Summa Theologica* (New York: McGraw-Hill, 1969), XVI, 157.

44   Aquinas, *De Virtutibus*, a. 12.

45   R.M. Schultes, "De Caritate Ut Forma Virtutum," *Divus Thomas*, XXXI (1928), 17.

46   Aquinas, *III Sent.*, d. 27, q. 1.

47   Horvath, *Caritas*, p. 159.

48   *Ibid.*, p. 160.

49   Aquinas, *III Sent.*, d. 27, q. 1.

50   Simonin, "Autour De La Solution," p. 180.

51   Ilien, *Wesen*, p. 97.

52   Aquinas, *ST*, I-II, 27,3.

53   Keller and Lavaud, "La Charité," p. 450.

54   Pépin, *La Charité*, p. 43.

55   Egenter, *Gottesfreundschaft*, p. 58.

56   Keller, "De Virtute Caritatis," p. 249.

57   *Ibid.*, p. 251.

Chapter III

The Virtues in the Service of
Friendship with God

The whole point of Aquinas's moral theology is to show us how to live so that the story of our life can have a happy ending.[1] But this means the story of our life has to be to be told a particular way. For Thomas did not think every human life, however told, would have a happy ending. And Thomas did not think we could make of our life whatever we wished and all would be well. No, the moral theology of the *Prima Secundae* is the eloquent confession of a man who believed the only lives that end happily are the ones that find happiness in God.

Christians try to live the story of God. Similarly, the moral theology of St. Thomas Aquinas argues we are not free to become whoever we want for we are called to become as much like God as we possibly can. We are called to become another Christ, to resemble God that severely. But this means we have to change. We have to become more than we already are. To live the story of God is the achievement of virtue because the virtues are the activities by which a self resplendent in godliness is acquired. For Thomas, goodness and happiness are internally connected to those activities by which we take on the character of God's friends. As chapter two presented, happiness is charity because charity is the love by which we acquire a resemblance to God sufficient for us to consider God another self. Charity is our happiness because through charity we not only become more than we already are, we become God's friend, another self to the God who is our joy.

The Christian moral life demands becoming a certain kind of person. In a sense, this is what happiness is. Happiness is the activity of the transformation of the self in goodness; in Christian language, happiness is the formation of the self in the goodness of God. More precisely, happiness is the work of charity's virtues because only activities expressive of such love can effect the transformation we need to become God's friends. The virtues are our means of perfection, the activities by which we become like God; however, the virtues perfect us not exactly because they move us towards our end, but because they change us according to our end. The virtues enable us to participate in our end because through them we are formed in its goodness. The virtues testify we want to possess our end as fully as possible. We want to become it, we want to be shaped and determined in its goodness. And the virtues enable us to do so because through them we are transformed according to what we love.

Actions give us access to our good, but we do not want our kinship with the good to fade. There has to be a way our intimacy with the good can be preserved, and that is the function of the virtues. Virtues sustain contact with our good first because the good, as we saw in chapter two, is internal to the activity of virtue, and secondly, because through the virtues the good we seek becomes a quality of our character, a determination of ourself. The virtues are our perfection because through them we are formed in the end we seek.

The purpose of this book is to demonstrate that the moral theology of the *Prima Secundae*, specifically the treatise on the passions, the virtues, and the Gifts of the Spirit, is best understood when interpreted from the perspective of charity. When charity becomes the interpretative key, a cohesiveness and interrelatedness accrues to the *Prima Secundae* that otherwise might not be discerned. In chapter two we examined how such a reading of the treatise on the passions illumines their importance, especially in connection to the virtues. The treatise on the passions demonstrates why everything in Thomas's moral theology turns on the quality of our love, and argues forcefully why, if God is our happiness, charity must be our sovereign love. In this chapter our strategy is the same. Obviously Thomas has an ethic of virtue, but we can only appreciate its importance, as well as its uniqueness, when we realize virtues function according to whatever happiness they serve. Consequently, we shall consider the virtues, but always from the viewpoint of charity, for it is only in light of that love and that happiness that how Thomas explains the virtues and why his is an ethic of virtue can be appreciated. We need the virtues to become friends of God, but the very fact that that is what we are trying to become demands a different, quite specific sense of the virtues. How charity makes us see the virtues differently and appreciate their importance even more is the subject of chapter three.

A. Why We Need the Virtues: The Importance of Habits in the Formation of the Self

Perhaps the most frightening discovery of the moral life is that we are capable of being many things. There is no assurance we will be good, no assurance we will make of ourselves what we ought. There is nothing to protect us from ourselves, nothing to stop us short of mistakes, nothing to keep us from self-sabotage. We may be good, but there is no guarantee of it. Nothing determines us to happiness and nothing, if we insist, will keep us from making ourselves bad.

It is this insight which underlies Thomas's insistence that we need the virtues to become good. We have the capacity to achieve the good that is our perfection, but we are not determined to it. We stand before our good, as Thomas puts it, "in the relation of potentiality to actuality," but we are not unswervingly directed to any one good, but are confronted by an array of goods each with the possibility of becoming our own. Aquinas's rationale for the virtues is not just that we can become more than we already are, but that we can become many different things. As Thomas says, by the virtues we need to dispose ourselves to some goods instead of others because it is "possible for the unactualized subject to actualize its potentialities in more than one way."[2] Thus, the first reason Aquinas says we need the virtues is to determine our will to the good, for until we develop a habit to the good our behavior lacks the consistency and facility necessary for making the good characteristic of all we do.[3] As Lottin says, virtue "a donc pour rôle de diminuer l'indétermination, l'indécision de la puissance et de l'amèner à une activité plus constante, mieux assurée, plus connaturelle."[4]

In his excellent study of the virtues, *Les Habitus: Leur Caractere Spirituel*, Roton makes the same point. He notes that human beings have a special end which is their happiness, but they are not directed to that end by any "law of necessity." There is nothing in human nature that makes them "infallibly" tend to that end; on the contrary, since diverse possibilities are open to them, in order to reach the end intended by God they have to dispose themselves to it by cultivating a habit which makes them prefer that end over others.[5] That is why it is true but insufficient to say the will naturally seeks the good. Since the good is manifold and since many things appear good to the will, the will must be determined by virtue to some good instead of others. As Thomas says,

> The will, by its nature as a faculty, tends towards the good that reason proposes. But because this good is capable of realization in many different ways, it is necessary that the will should tend, by a disposition, to some particular good proposed by reason so that it may act more promptly."[6]

In short, because we can become so many different things, we must, through the virtues, dispose and determine ourselves to the one thing which allows us to achieve our end. Roton explains:

> A son tour, la forme est orientée vers l'opération. Si l'être n'est déterminé qu'à une seule opération en vertu de sa forme, il s'y porte naturellement de lui-même, ainsi les forces de la nature par elles-mêmes sont déterminées en un seul sens. Si au contraire il y a possibilité de réalisations multiples, l'indétermination des puissances d'action doit être levée par quelques dispositions particulières surajoutées....Mais l'homme n'est déterminé ni à un genre d'objets, ni à une manière de les atteindre....Mais, en ce qui le caractérise dans sa vie proprement humaine, l'homme a des puissances de grande envergure, qui sont d'elles-mêmes indéterminées. Ces puissances lui sont données pour vivre, penser, et agir en homme; elles doivent commander toute son activité humaine; il faut donc qu'elles soient orientées en ce sens. Si la nature

ne le fait pas, complètement du moins, le sujet humain devra se donner lui-même des dispositions, des déterminations, ou bien il en recevra, par un don spécial, de son créateur, pour accomplir des opérations d'un ordre plus élevé.[7]

The other reasons Thomas says we need virtues are "that a perfect operation be readily performed" and "that a perfect operation be performed with delight."[8] A virtuous person not only does good promptly and easily, but he also does good pleasingly because goodness describes who he is. That fulsome identification between the agent and his activity enables the virtuous person to perform readily and find joy in those activities which most befit the good. As Thomas says, "A man who is habituated in a given way inevitably finds those things delightful which have been made congenial to him by habit; by repetition and habituation they have become second nature to him."[9]

What is noteworthy about that passage is not just that a good person is one who delights in doing good, but that such a capacity can only be acquired through repeated, habitual activity. Thomas's point should not be missed. Surely it is easier to do good when we are good; however, by connecting the possibility of being good with the acquisition of habits and maintaining it is only by "repetition and habituation" that we become good, Thomas argues that being good is something we are neither naturally nor easily. We are only good by habit, by the painstaking and steady repetition of actions through which we take on qualities we did not have before. To recognize we become good through habit is an extremely important moral insight because it underscores that only doing good makes us good. We have no natural affinity with the good. It is hard for us to be good, and that is why initially we are clumsy in doing good. Initially, there is a strangeness to doing good-the good does not yet befit us-because we are not yet good ourselves.

Becoming good is a matter of practice. It takes an awfully long time to become genuinely good. Until we are truly virtuous being good will remain difficult, even alien, for we will lack the correspondence between virtuous actions and virtuous agents that is necessary for making being good not only second nature, but delightful. In short, the virtues make the moral life a history, a saga of the kind of ongoing growth and development necessary for goodness to be a quality of all activity. That we need habits to enable us to do the good readily and delightfully suggests not only that goodness is not natural to us, but also that such virtuosity is impossible without a history of activity which steadily turns us to the good.

But it is also hard to be determined to the good because developing a virtue often means overcoming a vice. A corollary reason we need habits to incline us to the good is because usually we already have an array of habits that turn us away from it. Good habits must be developed because bad habits must be overcome. This makes the necessity for virtues all the more apparent, but it also makes acquiring them all the more difficult because, at least initially, virtue must work to rehabilitate a will crippled by vice. True, Thomas does say the will is indeterminate to any one good, but that does not deny the will may already be deeply determined to something bad, to something which makes doing good not only arduous, but distasteful. In short, we may be dominated by disordered loves. As Roton comments, one reason developing good habits is toilsome is that before good habits can be acquired so many contrary dispositions must be dislodged.[10]

Thomas agrees. In the *Tertia Pars* he writes: "Sometimes after the first act of penitence, which is contrition, certain other effects of sin remain, dispositions developed by previous acts of sin, which make for some difficulty for the penitent to prefer acts of virtue."[11] "Therefore, there is no reason why," he continues, "once sin has been forgiven, certain dispositions caused from previous acts may not remain."[12] Thus, it is only through good habits that we become good, and this is true not just because habitually doing good determines us to the good, but also because it is only through cultivating good habits that their contraries can be weakened and destroyed. To say we become good through good habits implies not just that virtue gives us a new quality, but that it works a moral transformation, a conversion, because it frees us from one kind of habit in order to be determined by another.

That habits effect us that deeply indicates a further and even more significant reason we need them. It is through habits that we are given a self. Being emerges in agency. Who we are is cultivated in what we do, first because our nature is an activity, and secondly, because it is only through activity that we are shaped in the good we take ourselves to be; thus, to be one thing instead of another, we have to act in a very particular way. As long as the will remains indeterminate, so do we because a self takes form, indeed is possible, only through the will habitually seeking one thing instead of another.

To be poised equally before many different things but to be disposed habitually to none is to lack the agency necessary for acquiring a self. In order to be, at least in a way that gives us character, we have to be something habitually. We have to settle for some good and rule out others because the quality necessary for being a self and sustaining the identity selfhood requires is mediated through our most consistent choices. In short, the condition for selfhood is agency disposed in a particular way. As Noble says, "La loi générale du développement humain" is "la loi de l'habitude."[13] The habits are necessary for becoming a self because a self, which is the particular determination of being and agency given by actions, emerges only through our willingness to behave consistently in a certain way.[14]

Habits shape the self because through them a person is given a quality or form. Thomas says habits are "qualities or forms which are possessed by a faculty and which give it a tendency to actions of one specific kind."[15] Habit comes from the Latin word 'habere', which means to have or possess something. To have a habit is to possess a quality or form which disposes the agent to act in a certain way.[16] Notice that Thomas's reasoning is necessarily circular. To be a self is to possess a quality or form in the will that makes something which was initially indeterminate determinate; that is, to be a self is to possess a quality by which we can be distinguished and identified. We become a self by taking on a certain form, but the form comes through the activity; thus, selfhood and character accrue to us by habitually acting in a certain way. We possess certain habits because of the form of our agency, but our agency is thus formed only because we have consistently acted according to the quality of the habit. As Gilson explains, a habit disposes us to act in one way rather than another. Actions are always in accord with a form. If we regularly act a certain way, the form of the action becomes the form of our agency, thus disposing us to act that way all the more.[17] Simply put, our habits make us who we are because to be a self is to possess a certain form, and the form of the self is mediated through the form of the action.

Action is internally connected to agency, and agency to action, to demonstrate that habits determine us neither superficially nor partially, but wholly and simply. Habits determine us. Habits give us a self. That is Aquinas's point. Lottin notes that Aquinas received his understanding of habit from Aristotle, and for Aristotle a habit was a quality that made a subject who she or he was, a quality that fixed or determined, for better or worse, one's very being.[18] Habits dispose not simply our actions, but also we who are the agents of those actions because the quality of the habit becomes the quality of the self. Roton says the principal role of the habits is to dispose "a being in itself" to good or evil, to enrich the self in goodness or to impoverish it in evil. It is the agent himself or herself who is determined one way or another.[19] That is why what we do figures so largely in who we are. Our self is whatever we habitually do because the quality or determination we give the self is a function of our most perduring activity.

Thus, it is not just that agency is connected to action, but that agency is action. Agency is distinguishable from action, but not separable from it because the self is not only through but also in its most habitual activities; therefore, being a self is being active in a habitual way. The reason for this is that a habit is a form of being. It is through habitual behavior, expressly the virtues, that we come to possess a self because virtue forms us according to the principle of its activity, namely, the good. This is why Roton says a habit "makes us be in a certain way." He explains:

> L'étymologie de l'habitus, entendu en ce sens, se tirerait donc mieux du verbe 'se habere' que du verbe 'habere'; il désigne la possession par un sujet non

point de quelque chose d'exterieur mais de lui-même tout d'abord; 'se habere' veut dire alors: se trouver dans une certaine disposition, se comporter en soi-même, ou à l'égard d'autre chose. Ou, mieux encore, si l'on préfère, le verbe 'habere' aurait ici le sens d'être: l'habitus est une forme d'être; et il pénètre si profondément son sujet qu'il est pour lui comme une seconde nature. On dit que l'artiste par exemple est maître de son art, cela ne signifie pas seulement qu'il en possède toutes les règles dont il use à la perfection, mais surtout que son art, véritable habitus, est quelque chose de lui-même, tellement que l'oeuvre reflète toujours les traits de son auteur. Cet avoir qui marque ainsi son sujet dans ce qu'il a de plus intime, le modifie, le détermine et constitute pour lui un état; il veut dire: être d'une certaine facon.[20]

These few preliminary reflections on the necessity of the virtues anchor charity even more firmly at the core of Thomas's moral theology for at least two reasons. First, given the indeterminacy of the will, if the goal of our life is to become godly a habit is needed to direct us consistently to a God we are not naturally or instinctively inclined to seek. That habit is charity. It would be a different matter if seeking God was something we naturally intended, but that is not how Thomas understands the will. The will has to be trained and disciplined. A determinate choosing of some goods instead of others has to be carved into the will, and that is what a habit works. To seek God in all things-for that is what friendship with God requires-the will has to be transformed from being undetermined to any one good, to being determined wholly and pleasingly to the consummate goodness of God. Charity has to be our most habitual activity and the formal principle of our will for unless our will is turned to seeking God there is no way the transformation of the self into a friend of God is possible.

Friendship with God is acquired. We become anything through habit, and God's friend is something we become only if the habit that formally determines our will is charity. Thomas's analysis of the habits underscores the absolute importance of charity because if habits are indispensable for us to become anything, charity is indispensable for us to be God's friend. Another habit makes us another kind of person. Only charity makes us God's friend, and becoming God's friend is a transformation only gradually achieved the more the will is determined to God.

We become God's friend by habit, and this suggests the second reason Aquinas's analysis of the habits strengthens the importance of charity-friendship as the center around which his moral theology has to be understood. As we noted in our examination of the habits, one reason we need to develop habits is that habits give us a self. The only way to be, we said, is to be habitually. But as soon as that is acknowledged, we see how crucial it is to be involved habitually in whatever good we take to comprise the fullness of our life. It is not just that our most habitual activity makes us, but that its effect on us is inescapable. What is mediated through activity is the form of whatever good the activity seeks, and as we noted in chapter two, the more we habitually act towards a specific good, the more we receive its form, the more we acquire its likeness.

That is why charity has to be the constitutive activity of our life. Charity has to be the habitual, perduring activity of the will-its formal principle-because charity is the only habit capable of making us like God. Yes, being emerges in agency, and if we want a self characterized by godliness, charity has to be the habit to which the will is determined. Activity determines us according to its form; consequently, if we are to be known by the goodness of God, charity must be the principle of all our actions. No other habit can make us God's friend because no other habit shares charity's form. A self comes to us by taking on a certain form. Our most persistent habit is a reflection of what we want our self to be. What Thomas's description of the habits assures us is that if we want to become a friend of God, charity must be the habit which determines the will and thus informs all we do. As we said, habit is a form of being, and charity alone is the habit capable of forming our being unto likeness with God, a likeness, in friendship's parlance, that makes God another self to us.

B. The Relationship Between the Virtues and the Telos: Why Charity Must be the Form of the Virtues

Still, up to this point there remains something curiously incomplete about our investigation of virtue. To speak of virtue as a habit which determines the will begs the question of precisely the specific good every virtue works to achieve. Virtues mean nothing in themselves because the meaning of every virtue is relative to the overriding good it is the purpose of virtue to achieve. A virtue is intelligible not in itself, but in light of the goal or telos to which it is to direct us. Similarly, while it is important to say we need the virtues in order to be a self, we have to say more because the kind of self formed by the virtues depends on the principal good those virtues seek. As we indicated at the outset of this chapter, the strategy of the virtues is to change us; however, if that is so we cannot understand the virtues fully until we specify the telos or end according to which that transformation of the self is to be measured. What a virtue does is allow us to participate in our end by becoming one with that end, and this is why a full assessment of the virtues cannot be given apart from specifying the end to which the virtues direct us. In short, to think about the virtues apart from the end they serve is to misunderstand them.

This is clearly Aquinas's understanding of the virtues. A virtue has meaning not in itself, but only in reference to the end to which it is meant to dispose us. Listen to how Thomas defines virtue: "A virtue is a good disposition...which makes an agent tend to act in accordance with its nature," and a vice is "a bad disposition...which makes it tend to act against its nature."[21] Aquinas takes his understanding of virtue from Aristotle,[22] who said "every virtue or excellence (1) renders good the thing itself of which it is the excellence, and (2) causes it to perform its function well."[23]

As Alasdair MacIntyre points out, what compels this understanding of virtue is an explicit view of what it means to be a person. Virtues change us, but for Aristotle and Aquinas they change us in a very exact, highly defined way. Something is a virtue only if the change it works corresponds to the telos the agent ought to achieve. As MacIntyre puts it, "Human beings, like members of all other species, have a specific nature; and that nature is such that they have certain aims and goals, such that they move by nature towards a specific telos."[24]

MacIntyre says that for Aristotle and Aquinas the virtues were tied to a conviction about what every human life ought to achieve. Virtues were necessary to fulfill that purpose; indeed they made it possible, for they alone were activities by which the good of human nature could be possessed. But this also presumed there was some single good, some indisputable function, that was a human being's purpose to fulfill. To be human was to be pursuing this telos; not to pursue it, or to choose some other goal, was to forsake one's humanity. Implicit in Aristotle's and Aquinas's definition of virtue is the conviction that the virtues are perfecting precisely because they are linked to a specific telos whose possession represents the intended purpose and fulfillment of every man and woman. For Aristotle and Aquinas, to speak of virtues apart from this telos would be unintelligbile for a specific activity is a virtue only if it directs the agent to the single end in which the perfection of human nature resides. Thus, every virtue is a virtue because its activity corresponds to the telos to which human life must tend if it is not to be frustrated. As MacIntyre explains, an account of the virtues always presupposes an account of a telos, an understanding of what men and women ought to be making of themselves so they can bring their lives to successful completion:

> Within that teleological scheme there is a fundamental contrast between man-as-he-happens-to-be and man-as-he-could-be-if-he-realized-his-essential-nature. Ethics is the science which is to enable men to understand how they make the transition from the former state to the latter. Ethics therefore on this view presupposes some account of potentiality and act, some account of the essence of man as a rational animal and above all some account of the human telos. The precepts which enjoin the various virtues and prohibit the vices which are their counterparts instruct us how to move from potentiality to act, how to realize our true nature and to reach our true end. To defy them will be to be frustrated and incomplete, to fail to achieve that good of rational happiness which it is peculiarly ours as a species to pursue.[25]

The connection MacIntyre sees both Aristotle and Aquinas forging between an account of the virtues and a corresponding account of a telos bolsters our argument that it is only clear why Thomas espouses an ethic of virtue and how this renders our perfection when his account of the virtues is read not separately, but in view of the friendship with God the virtues are meant to serve. As MacIntyre explains, "A virtue is, as with Aristotle, a quality the exercise of which leads to the achievement of the human telos."[26] A virtue is a means to this end insofar as "the virtues are precisely those qualities the possession of which will enable an individual to achieve eudaimonia and the lack of which will frustrate his movement toward that telos."[27]

Thus, the virtues enable our perfection, but which activities are perfecting cannot be determined prior to specifying the telos. The telos gives any virtue its meaning. "It is the telos of man as a species," MacIntyre says, "which determines what human qualities are virtues."[28] A different understanding of what that telos is will call for another set of virtues because what differentiates a virtue from other activities is this connection to the end in which human fullness is taken to reside. A virtue is an activity which enables the agent to share in and be formed by his or her telos; consequently, the relationship between the virtues and a telos must be spied because the identity of any virtue is secondary to and contingent upon the end which is a virtue's purpose to attain. This is why MacIntyre says for Aristotle and Aquinas

> the good life for man is prior to the concept of a virtue in just the way in which on the Homeric account the concept of a social role was prior. Once again it is the way in which the former concept is applied which determines how the latter is to be applied. In both cases the concept of virtue is a secondary concept.[29]

This is why for Thomas the virtues take their meaning from charity. Charity illumines the purpose of the virtues because friendship with God is the end for which every virtue exists. Any account of the virtues presupposes a telos that defines those virtues' meaning, and for Thomas that telos is charity-friendship with God. MacIntyre notes that "Aristotle takes the telos to be a certain kind of life; the telos is not something to be achieved at some future point, but in the way our whole life is construed."[30] The same is true for Thomas. Thomas did not understand friendship with God to be a beatitude reserved wholly beyond this world, but to indicate what our being in this world means. To say a Christian's telos is the beatitude of perfect friendship with God is to make a corresponding claim about the shape human life must take. A telos gives life a special construction. More exactly, a telos is a kind of life because as soon as we tend toward a good as our end, our life gets formed according to it. If friendship with God is that end, then the activities of such a life-its virtues-must not only be directed to it, but also formed according to it. In other words, a telos is a way of life because it is not just an end, but activity toward an end. A telos is the virtues displayed in a certain way. Put more strongly, the telos is not consequent to virtue or extrinsic to virtue, but is internal to the activity of virtue. In a helpful summary, Roton says:

> L'habitus au contraire qualifie toujours par rapport à la fin de l'être, c'est-à-dire par rapport à sa nature qui est déjà en quelque sorte sa fin, ou par rapport a son action qui en sera le perfectionnement. L'habitus est toujours une disposition heureuse ou malheureuse par rapport à une fin....En somme, l'habitus, comme toute disposition, a pour rôle de régler intrinsèquement un sujet quel qu'il soit, dans se nature ou ses facultés, de facon à créer en elles un état de convenance ou de non-convenance à l'égard d'une forme qui est le bien de ce sujet.[31]

We should understand Aquinas's sense of virtue in the same way. He says virtue is "a suitable disposition of a given thing with reference to its nature," and includes the definition of Aristotle: "'Virtue is a disposition of a perfect thing to that which is best, and by perfect I mean that which is disposed according to nature.' "[32] By nature, Thomas does not mean a static, unchanging, already possessed totality, but being virtuous in a way that furthers friendship with God. Our nature is to be virtuous, it is to be active according to and for the sake of our most proper function, that of being friends with God. This is what Thomas means when he speaks of the virtues as "activity-directed states" and of our nature as "a goal of production and change."[33] The virtues are connected with our nature because human nature is an operation, the continual tending toward the telos in which human perfection resides. To be human is to be active for the sake of whatever good is understood to bring our nature to its fullest possible development. In short, a virtue has to be perfecting because the very thing which makes a virtue active is its intrinsic ordination to the end that is our nature's perfection. As Aquinas explains, "Intrinsically, every disposition is in some way connected with action. For every disposition has an intrinsic relationship to the nature of its possessor, whether it accords with that nature or conflicts with it."[34]

To say that the virtues dispose us to the goal of our nature is to acknowledge that the virtues are our perfection because through them we participate in and are increasingly conformed to our telos. The virtues are connected to our nature through the category of form, and as activities they are perfecting because what specifically distinguishes the virtues from other activities is that they take their form from the consummate good of our nature. This is why the telos is internal to the activity of virtue, and it is also why the agent develops in the likeness of her good in the measure that she is virtuous. Since the telos is what forms the virtues, the more she is virtuous the more she is united to what she loves.

This is how Thomas explains it. "The nature of a thing," which is its most proper function or operation, "is indeed brought to completion by a form; but in order to acquire a form the subject needs to be in the appropriate state. Again, the form itself has a relation to an action which is either a goal or the means to a goal."[35] Men and women are perfected by being formed in their telos-by possessing charity's form-but, as Thomas indicates, we have access to this form only through virtuous activity. We have to be virtuous in order to be happy because the virtues bear the form of the happiness we seek. But we are the agents of our actions, and action is internally connected to agency; therefore, we are "brought to completion" by virtue because through such activity the form of our perfection qualifies and determines us as agents. "La génération d'un habitus," Roton explains, "est le fait de l'introduction d'une forme en un sujet, par la connaturalisation de celui-ci avec cette forme...."[36] Like any habit, a virtue modifies or changes the agent by giving her a quality she did not have before. What distinguishes virtues from other habits is that the quality introduced in the agent is the form of the good that is her end. In short, virtue perfects by giving us charity's form.

As Thomas says, "To modify something, according to St. Augustine, is to make it accord with a standard. So a modification is an actualization of something which accords with a certain standard."[37] For Thomas, that standard is God because the purpose of every virtue is to transfigure us in the especial goodness of God. Virtue's rationale is to allow us to achieve our end. As this passage suggests, for Thomas we achieve that end by being changed and modified according to the goodness of God, and thus attain enough likeness to God to share the happiness of God.

Aquinas's claim that charity is the form of the virtues can be interpreted as making the same point. To say that charity informs all the virtues and that there can be no true virtue that is not born from charity's love means that charity is both internal to and intrinsic to the definition of every virtue. It means any activity is formally defined as a virtue only when shaped by charity's love. Thomas broaches this point when he says,

> As already stated, virtue is ordered to the good. Now the good is realized principally in an end, for whatever is subordinated to an end is said to be good only with reference to it....For man the ultimate and principal good is the enjoyment of God, according to the verse in the Psalms, 'But for me it is good to be near God,' and to this end he is directed by charity....It is obvious then that true virtue, without any qualification, is directed to man's principal good; as Aristotle puts it, virtue is what 'disposes a thing already perfectly constituted in its nature to its maximum achievement.' And so taken, there can be no true virtue without charity.[38]

As Gilson comments, "To be a virtue is to be really a virtue, that is, to satisfy the definition of a virtue,"[39] and that is what Thomas claims here. By definition, a virtue enables the achievement of an end. It is through virtue that we move to our end. If, as Thomas continues, the telos of human life is God, and that is the work of charity's love, then that charity must be the form of the virtues is entailed by the definition of virtue, namely, that it "disposes a thing already perfectly constituted to its maximum achievement." As Gillemann says, "An act has no meaning if it does not point to an end, and finally to the ultimate end. In the Christian, the act will reach the ultimate end under the influence of charity."[40] Every virtue needs charity as its form because it is only the activity of that special love that is capable of referring all our actions to God. Yes, something is only a virtue if it is really a virtue, that is, if it satisfies virtue's purpose of perfecting us unto our end. For people whose end is God, the virtues must be formed from charity because any other principle of activity would not only stop short of God, but also make them something other than godly.

That every virtue needs charity does not mean, Gillemann is careful to add, that every virtue is charity. "Charity is called the form of all virtuous acts," he explains, "not as being their exemplar or their essential form," which would make charity the only virtue, "but rather as an efficient cause, insofar as it sets the form on all,"[41] a position which parallels Aquinas's own.[42] Thomas does not want the notion of charity as form of the virtues to be interpreted in such a way that charity threatens the material identity or proper species of each virtue, for every virtue has its own proper object and its own proper act; however, he does mean, Gillemann insists, that every virtue needs charity's form because "charity gives these acts, really and intrinsically, their supernatural moral perfection, their concrete moral form, by ordering them to its own end."[43] He concludes,

> And when we say that charity gives to all the commanded acts its own proper form, we mean that it makes them participate in its own specific perfection, that of touching God; in this also consists the supernatural perfection of the human act of the just.[44]

C. How Charity Forms the Virtues

This is how Thomas develops his argument that charity is the form of the virtues. As Schultes says, the key principle for Thomas is that the form of an act is taken from its end: "In actibus voluntariis id quod est ex parte finis, est formale."[45] This principle follows Aquinas's understanding of the will as an appetite. As we saw in chapter two, the will is an appetite which tends to whatever it most loves, but because the activity of the will begins not with itself, but with the good which elicits its response, the activity of the will is formally identified according to that good. Moreover, because the love which moves the will is a passion, the will is active only in virtue of receiving the form of the thing loved. In other words, Thomas's claim that charity forms the virtues is entailed by his analysis of how the will functions as both passion and appetite.

In the *Prima Secundae*, Thomas says the specific character of any action "comes from the side of the object, which shapes the activity and determines the form it takes,"[46] and that since "the object of will is being an end and good...it is clear that this is the determining principle of human acts as such....So then we may add that the end also provides moral acts with their proper specific character."[47] The form of an action comes from the end because it is to the end that the will tends. That the "object of will is being an end and good" means only that the activity of the will is neither sporadic nor intermittent; rather, the will is constantly and actively related to that in which the agent sees his or her perfection. It is a relationship of love, an ongoing tending toward and availing of oneself to the good that is lacking for one's completion.

Because the activity of the will is love and because love is a passion, through that activity the form of the end gradually becomes the form of the agent. The more the agent is related to his or her good, the more the agent acquires the form of the good, and the more the form of the good is the agent's own, the more he or she not only acts for the sake of that good, but also in the manner of that good. As Thomas says, "For what a thing does reflects what its active self is; and since a thing is active in virtue of its form, its effect must bear a likeness to that form"[48] Because of the connection between agency and action, the subject acts increasingly in virtue of its end. Acting for the sake of the end gives an agent the quality of that end; in short, a "thing's active self" is whatever good in which it is most involved. Aquinas's analysis of form hinges on his understanding of love. That is why in his *Commentary on the Sentences* he says to claim a thing acts according to its form is to claim that it acts according to what it loves:

Unumquodque autem agit secundum exigentiam suae formae quae est principium agendi et regula operis. Bonum autem amatum est finis. Finis autem est principium in operabilibus sicut principia prima in cognoscendis.... ita amans cujus affectus est informatus ipso bono quod habet rationem finis, quamvis non sempter ultimi, inclinatur per amorem ad operandum secundum exigentiam amati.[49]

Acts are always formed from what one loves, and that is why charity forms the acts of those who love God. Charity is the form of every virtue not just because it is only when bearing charity's form that these acts reach God; rather, charity forms the virtues because the acts of one whose primary love is for God are always shaped according to God. Form is a matter of desire, and if a man and a woman really desire God, then this passion for God, whether explicit or not, is the strategy behind all they do. Charity forms the virtues of the person who loves God because every act is at the service of what one loves. It is unavoidable. What we love directs the will. Through this relationship of love the form of the end becomes the form of the one who loves. A similarity results, a kinship exists. Ultimately, charity is the form of the virtues because friendship for God is a question of character, a question of the kind of person such love creates. Virtues bear charity's form because it is from a friend of God that they proceed. The virtues are inseparable from charity because every virtue is determined by and at the service of whatever functions as our sovereign love. Every virtue is formed from the activity of our primary love, and if that is a love for God, they bear charity's form. Thomas summarizes:

In moral matters the form of an act is taken chiefly from its end, the reason being that the principle of moral acts is the will, of which the object, and in a sense, the form is the end. But the form of an action always follows that of the agent which produces it. Hence in morals what gives an act its reference to an end must also give it form. Now it is evident from what has been said already, that charity directs the acts of all the other virtues to our final end. Accordingly it shapes all these acts and to this extent is said to be the form of the virtues, for virtues themselves are so called with reference to 'formed' acts.[50]

The formative influence of charity is an implication of Thomas's understanding of intention. Intention resides in the will and describes the foremost purpose of the will in all its activity. Every-

thing an agent does both reflects and works for what the agent
fundamentally intends, for as the word suggests, to 'intend' something is to be turned toward it and to seek it. Intention is moral
language describing the fundamental desire of the agent, and it is a
word which reveals that what an agent most desires is the formal
element in all she does. Aquinas notes that because "the will moves
the other powers to their activity with respect to executive motion
considered as coming from the side of the subject," thus expressing
what the agent intends, "the ends they achieve, as being particular
goods, are comprehended in the will's object."[51]   Everything the
will does is comprehended in what the will intends because each instance of activity expresses the ruling interest of the will. Lottin
captures this well. He says it is intention "qui actionne toute notre
vie, mobilise efficacement nos puissances....L'influence de cette intention du bien moral est capitale: l'intention commande toute la
vie...."[52] In question twelve of the *Prima Secundae*, Aquinas elaborates:

> Consequently, intention belongs first and foremost to the power which sets
> up a motion to an end; thus we speak of an architect or director in charge
> moving others by his command to the end he intends. We have shown that it
> is the will which moves all the other powers of the soul to an end. And so it is
> evident that intention, properly speaking, is an act of will...when the end is re-
> garded as the final term beyond something directed towards it, and the word
> for this is intention.[53]

And so if charity is in the will that intention is virtually present in
all the agent does. Intending friendship with God is the most
definitive activity of the one who loves God; therefore, since the
form of an act is taken from its end, every act proceeds from the
will to deepen the agent's participation in his lovelife with God.
This is why Aquinas speaks of charity as the "principle of all the
virtues, insofar as it moves them all to their end,"[54] or as "the form
of all the virtues in that every act of all the virtues is ordered to the
highest good that is loved...."[55] What a person intends will inform
all she or he does because intention describes the active way we are
related to whatever we love most. We are related to our end by intending it, and that relationship is the context in which all our ac-

tivity has meaning because everything we do is subservient to the love relationship which is our life. As Lottin notes, this intention is formal to all activity, not in the sense that every virtue is charity, but inasmuch as every virtue is formed from within charity's desire. Charity, he says,

> pénètre donc, à la manière d'une 'intention virtuelle', les actes de toutes les autres vertus. Cette pénetratration qui, par définition, est inhérente à ces actes, n'affecte cependant pas leur substance à la manière d'une forme substantielle; mais elle leur donne l'existence et les meut vers la fin dernière.[56]

Thomas sometimes expresses this influence of charity on all the other virtues by saying that charity "moves" or "commands the acts of all the virtues" to its end.[57] This captures the effect of charity on all the agent does, but it can be misleading if it implies that every virtue, though under the direction of charity, acts apart from or even subsequent to charity. If so, this would mean that the influence of charity is extrinsic to the activity of the other virtues. But that cannot be since charity is an expression of agency, and action and agency are internally connected.

Aquinas better describes the relationship between charity and the other virtues through the metaphor of conception, wherein charity is the "mother" from which all the virtues proceed:

> Charity is called the end of the other virtues because it directs them all to its own end. And since a mother is one who conceives in herself from another, charity is called the mother of the other virtues, because from desire of the ultimate end it conceives their acts by charging them with life.[58]

Thus, as a mother gives birth to her child, every virtue is born from charity's love. The advantage of this analogy is that it keeps intact the internal connection between charity and the other virtues. To say there can be no virtue without charity is to recognize no virtue operates apart from charity. As Aquinas's metaphor suggests, every virtue is "conceived" from or brought forth from charity's love, and that means every virtue is formed from within and expressive of the love relationship we have with God. Each virtue is birthed from charity and that means charity is the necessary condition of every virtue not in the sense that its activity is prior to the other virtues, but that it is precisely from within the crucible of charity's friendship that every other virtue is formed.

Sometimes Thomas expresses this intrinsic relationship between charity and the other virtues through the idea of 'participation'. By this he means a virtue is perfected not through activity independent of charity, but through participation in charity's love. In the *Commentary on the Sentences*, he writes: "Similiter etiam patet quod est forma perficiens unamquamque virtutem in ratione virtutis. Inferior enim potentia non habet perfectionem virtutis nisi secundum quod participat perfectionem potentiae superioris....[59] A virtue cannot achieve its end lest wrought from the very love its activity is to deepen. There is an intrinsic ordering of every virtue to charity, not in the sense that every virtue is charity, but that it is a virtue in the measure it has participated in and emerges from charity's love. Falanga captures this well when he speaks of the virtues "participating in the mode proper to charity,"[60] insofar as the form charity provides is the activity of friendship itself, the reciprocal exchange of love between the Christian and God. And this is what Gillemann implies when he writes that "charity is the exemplary form of all virtue, but it is an effective exemplar producing the virtues,"[61] because no virtue can reach charity's end unless it is modeled on and produced from charity's love. Lottin puts this even more directly when he suggests each virtue receives its being and its own particular perfection through its participation in charity:

> On peut donc dire que la charité est forme exemplaire, 'forma exemplaris'; non pas qu'elle soit un simple modèle, comme un être de la nature est modèle pour le peintre, mais en ce sens que c'est en participant à sa perfection qu'une chose reçoit l'être, 'per cuius participationem aliquid habet esse.[62]

The strategy of this chapter has been to demonstrate why Thomas's account of the virtues cannot be appreciated apart from charity. We began our argument by sketching why we need the virtues to be good, underscoring the importance of habits, and emphasizing that one whose end is God must be habitually inclined to God through charity. Next, we tightened the connection between charity and the other virtues by studying the relationship between the virtues and their telos. We stressed especially that virtues are secondary categories that derive their meaning from their end; therefore, virtues cannot be understood apart from the telos they serve for it is in bearing the form of the telos that they are virtues. We concluded with an analysis of Thomas's claim that charity is the form of the virtues. To claim this is to recognize there can be no true virtue without charity because every virtue is formed from charity's love. The friendship love of charity produces or gives birth to every virtue, and Aquinas expresses this by saying every virtue is formed from a participation in charity's love, a conclusion which warrants our claim that the virtues must be understood in service of the love which begets them.

In the last section of the chapter we want to complete this argument by suggesting the connection Thomas forges between charity-friendship with God and all the other virtues calls for a special understanding of how we consider a virtue's measure or standard of goodness. In short, if there is no true virtue without charity, then not only will the formal principle of charity, the goodness and love of God, mark the rule of every virtue, but the meaning of a virtue will also vary according to the friendship we have achieved with God, the deeper and more abiding the friendship, the more perfectly the virtue will be displayed.

D. Why God is the Measure of a Virtue's Goodness

Consider how a virtue is said to grow or increase. Roton observes that virtue increases not by quantity, as if one could have a greater abundance or surplus of a virtue, but by the subject being increasingly determined by the virtue's form. A growth or increase of virtue is measured in terms of how a person is more fully and habitually characterized by that virtue's activity, and thus possessed by its form. Roton notes that Thomas used many phrases to explain the increase of virtue in the agent. He spoke of a "reduction from imperfect to perfect," of a "greater participation of the subject in the form," or of a "greater rooting of the form in the subject." Referring to an analogy employed by Aquinas, Roton says just as a tree grows by being rooted more deeply in the soil, "ainsi l'habitus augmente, s'intensifie, dans la mesure ou il pénètre plus profondément la potentialité du sujet, où il s'installe davantage in lui. C'est par ce mode d'union de l'habitus à son sujet qu'il faut expliquer la croissance de l'habitus."[63]

What this analogy infers is that virtue grows from within the more an agent is determined by and at one with a virtue's activity, that is, the more firmly and wholly the agent is qualified by the virtue's goodness. Virtue's growth is internal, not external because virtue bespeaks a quality of the end, and a virtue is more fully possessed in the measure that the form of the virtue inheres more deeply in the agent. As Roton explains, virtue grows the more an agent is given over to its form, for it is in being possessed by this form that the end which is the agent's perfection is more perfectly the principle of all the agent does:

> Le sujet joue le rôle de matiére vis-à-vis de la forme, il est en puissance vis-à-vis de cet acte; il n'aura par conséquent union que dans la mesure où l'actualité de la forme triomphera de la potentialité du sujet. Et si le sujet est en puissance à des formes diverses et opposées, plus sa potentialité sera réduite et déterminée par une seule forme, plus on pourra le considére comme ne faisant qu'un avec cette forme, plus il la possédera parfaitement et plus on dira que la forme s'est dévelopée. La qualité s'accroit ainsi quand s'y ajoute ce qui manque au sujet qui la possède imparfaitement; or, ce qui manque au sujet dans cet état, ce n'est pas l'entité de la qualité, mais la perfection dans cette qualité....[64]

But since charity is the form of the virtues and a virtue increases the more a subject is given over to its form, that implies that the sense or meaning of a virtue changes the deeper one's friendship grows with God. The meaning of a virtue is never constant because our possession of a virtue's excellence increases relative to our friendship with God. The perfection of a virtue is measured by its most excellent activity, but a virtue's excellence is a function of how completely an agent has been determined by its form; therefore, the more one succumbs to friendship with God, the deeper is their possession of a virtue and the greater is their display of that virtue's excellence.

Thomas suggests this when he distinguishes between the purifying or intermediate virtues of those "still on their way," and the perfect virtues of those who "have already arrived." In both cases the names of the virtues are the same, but the sense and meaning of the virtues changes according to one's nearness to God. To be near God is to be like God, it is to approximate the goodness of God by having God's goodness as the formal principle of our own. The deeper and more penetrating our friendship with God, the more our goodness resembles God's. The more in friendship with God we are transformed by God's love, the more all our actions are formed from the goodness by which all things are good. A virtue's perfection depends on the love that forms it. This is why the virtues are displayed differently in holy people, in the friends of God we call saints. Virtues are stretched to their perfection in the saints because God's love has so perfectly transfigured their own, becoming the form and principle of all they do. In a telling passage, Aquinas explains how the meaning of a virtue grows and changes according to the likeness to God a Christian has attained.

> The intermediate virtues are distinguished by the difference between moving and having arrived, so that some are virtues of men who are on their way and striving towards likeness to God, and these are called purifying virtues. Thus prudence of this kind, by looking at the things of God, scorns the things of this world, and directs all its thoughts only to divine truths; temperance sets aside the needs of the body so far as nature allows; courage prevents the soul from being afraid about losing the body in its approach to heavenly things; and justice consists in the soul's giving a whole-hearted consent to following the course thus resolved.

> Besides these there are the virtues of those who have already achieved a likeness to God: these are called the virtues of 'an already purified spirit.' And then prudence sees only the things of God; temperance knows no earthly desires; courage is immune from passion; and justice, by imitating the divine mind, is united thereto in an everlasting covenant. Such are the virtues of the blessed, or in this life, of those who are at least at the summit of perfection.[65]

If the excellence of a virtue is approached the more it is formed in the goodness of its end, then the rule or measure of a virtue must be the goodness of God. A virtue's perfection increases the more a person through friendship with God has come to resemble God. The closer we are to God-the deeper and more penetrating our friendship-the more our virtues change because our character is more wholly determined by the love and goodness of God. Charity forms the virtues, but charity forms us too. It is God's friendship love acting within us, changing us, transforming us in God's goodness. The more God's goodness is our own, the more excellent our activities will be. Put differently, charity is the form of a virtue inasmuch as it is the principle of a virtue's excellence. But charity is also the love that makes us like God; therefore, a virtue's goodness is in proportion to a person's godliness. In this respect, the saints, the very ones who seem so unlike us, are the ones in whom the virtues are normatively displayed and the people against whom our own goodness must be measured.

The connection Thomas makes between a virtue's goodness and its formation in charity qualifies how we speak about the rule or measure of virtue. Typically it is held that an act is good if it is reasonable because reason is the distinguishing mark of human nature, and men and women become good if they act in accord with their nature.[66] As Lottin puts it, "La règle des actes humain...est la droite raison....Or, la forme qui constitue l'homme en sa nature d'homme c'est la raison."[67] An act is good if it is reasonable because, it is argued, men and women are reasonable; thus, reasonable acts best represent the function and purpose of human nature. At times, Thomas adopts this position. An act's reasonableness determines its goodness because to act reasonably is to act in a way befitting one's nature, and that is the purpose of virtue. For example, in *De Virtutibus*, Thomas says: "For since man is human because he has reason, the good for man must be according to reason."[68] And in the *Summa*, Thomas asserts that "clearly the good of moral virtue consists in fitting the measure of reason."[69]

But Thomas's remarks must be interpreted in light of their context. When he speaks of reason as the rule of virtue, Thomas has in mind virtues which dispose the agent to a purely human or natural end. The rule of a virtue must be taken from the good it is the purpose of virtue to attain. If men and women are considered purely in their natural state with no telos beyond this world, then reason suffices as a standard for goodness; however, once the telos is not this world but the Kingdom of God, then a different standard of goodness is required. The standard of a virtue is whatever good the virtue needs to achieve. Its goodness then is measured not primarily in its reasonableness, but in its fittingness to its end, for it is the telos to which virtues are directed that determines what makes them good. The more they enable an agent's participation in her end, the more we can call them good.

This is why Thomas says the rule of a virtue's goodness must be taken from the virtue's end. Different purposes make for different standards of goodness. If we think of men and women called to be citizens of this world, then reason is the measure of virtue because acts which are reasonable allow the optimum development of those whose telos does not exceed life in the world. But if we think of men and women gifted with the possibility of friendship with God, then the standard of virtue is not human reasonableness, but the goodness of God. Since God is our telos, our ultimate and consummate good, God is the One by whom a virtue's goodness must be gauged. Thomas writes:

> Human acts possess goodness inasmuch as they fit their due rule and measure; and consequently human virtue, the principle of all a man's good actions, consists in reaching to this norm. Now this, as already shown, is twofold, the human reason and God himself. Therefore as moral virtue is defined as being according to right reason, even so, reaching to God strikes the essential note of virtue, as we have seen with faith and hope.[70]

And again,

> Since goodness in human acts comes from their matching their due norm, human virtue, which is a principle of good acts, must lie in reaching this standard. Now, as already mentioned, there is a twofold standard, namely, the human reason and God, and God is the first against which human reason is to be measured.[71]

Thomas's argument supports our thesis that it is only in view of charity that we have any idea of how the virtues function for Thomas or what they possibly mean. It is charity that makes a virtue good, charity that accounts for a virtue's perfection, because the overriding strategy of Thomas's moral theology is to make us friends of God, and the transformation of the self unto a friend of

God can only succeed when the virtues bear a love capable of making us godly. A virtue is good inasmuch as it succeeds its purpose, and it does this by bearing the form of its end; therefore, God is the rule of virtue, the standard of a virtue's excellence, because virtues whose formal principle is God render a likeness to God which is beatitude's perfection.   Every virtue is perfected in the friendship with God it serves. The connection between charity and the virtues is unbreakable because union with God in friendship is the goal of the Christian moral life, and only virtues which are formed from charity can achieve it. This is why Van Ouwerkerk says charity must be the substantial norm of Christian morality:

> La charité est la norme substantielle de la vie morale surnaturelle. La vie chrétienne est premièrement et substantiellement l'union de la charité avec Dieu, et le caractère chrétien, quelque forme qu'il adopte, est toujours une détermination ultérieure de cette union et, par conséquent, de cette norme substantielle.[72]

The point of this chapter has been important in furthering the central argument of the book, namely, that the moral theology of the *Prima Secundae*, especially the treatise on the virtues, can be more fully and properly appreciated when read in light of charity-friendship with God. When examined from the perspective of charity, it is clear that everything in Thomas's moral theology stands in service of this premier love. That is why we suggested not only that the account of the virtues cannot be read apart from the account of the passions, but also that the virtues cannot be separated from the Gifts of the Spirit, for when our passion is for God it is in the Gifts of the Spirit that our virtues are perfected. Too often Aquinas's treatise on the Gifts has been either ignored or read as extraneous to the virtues, a mere appendage to a moral theology already complete. But that is not so. Once the virtues are refracted in light of charity, the Gifts of the Spirit are impossible to ignore; indeed, they describe the virtues of one whose friendship with God is so complete that the Spirit is the active principle of all she does. The Gifts of the Spirit are the perfection of charity's virtues, and we shall consider them next.

Notes

1 Gilson, *Moral Values*, p. 19.

2 Aquinas, *ST*, I-II, 49,4.

3 Aquinas, *De Virtutibus*, a. 1.

4 Dom Odon Lottin, *Morale Fondamentale* (Tournai: Desclée and Cie, 1954), p. 347.

5 Placide de Roton, *Les Habitus: Leur Caractère Spirituel* (Paris: Labergerie, 1934), p. 19.

6 Aquinas, *ST*, I-II, 50,6.

7 Roton, *Les Habitus*, pp. 15-16.

8 Aquinas, *De Virtutibus*, a. 1.

9 Aquinas, *ST*, I-II, 78,2.

10 Roton, *Les Habitus*, pp. 42-43.

11 Aquinas, *ST*, III, 89,1.

12 Aquinas, *ST*, III, 86,5.

13 Henri Noble, "Synthèse de La Doctrine Morale de Saint Thomas," *Saint Thomas d'Aquin: Sa Sainteté, Sa Doctrine Spirituelle*, cd. Leopold Lavaud (Saint-Maximin: Éditions de la Vie Spirituelle), p. 56.

14 For this idea of self, understood as the character or determination we give ourself through our actions, see Stanley Hauerwas, *Character and the Christian Life: A Study in Theological Ethics* (San Antonio: Trinity University Press, 1975), pp. 11-18.

15 Aquinas, *ST*, I-II, 54,1.

16 Aquinas, *ST*, I-II, 49,1.

17 Gilson, *Moral Values*, p. 138.

18 Lottin, *Morale Fondamentale*, p. 346.

19 Roton, *Les Habitus*, p. 25.

20 *Ibid*., p. 22.

21 Aquinas, *ST*, I-II, 54,3.

22 Aquinas, *ST*,I-II, 71,1.

23 Aristotle, *Ethics*, 1106a15-17.

24 Alasdair MacIntyre, *After Virtue* (Notre Dame, Indiana: University of Notre Dame Press, 1981), p. 139.

25 *Ibid*., p. 50.

26 *Ibid*., p. 172.

27 *Ibid*., p. 139.

28 *Ibid*., p. 172.

29 *Ibid*., p. 173.

30 *Ibid*., p. 163.

31 Roton, *Les Habitus*, p. 30.

32 Aquinas, *ST*, I-II, 71,1.

33 Aquinas, *ST*, I-II, 49,2.

34 Aquinas, *ST*, I-II, 49,3.

35 Aquinas, *ST*, I-II, 51,3.

36   Roton, *Les Habitus*, p. 96.

37   Aquinas, *ST*, I-II, 49,2.

38   Aquinas, *ST*, II-II, 23,7.

39   Gilson, *The Christian Philosophy*, pp. 340-341.

40   Gerard Gillemann, *The Primacy of Charity in Moral Theology*, trans. William F. Ryan and Andre Vachon (Westminster, Maryland: The Newman Press, 1959), pp. 30-31.

41   *Ibid*, p. 35.

42   Aquinas, *ST*, II-II, 23,8.

43   Gillemann, *The Primacy of Charity*, p. 35.

44   *Ibid*, p. 34.

45   R.M. Schultes, "De Caritate," p. 19.

46   Aquinas, *ST*, I-II, 9,1.

47   Aquinas, *ST*, I-II, 9,1.

48   Aquinas, *ST*, I, 4,3.

49   Aquinas, *III Sent.*, d. 27, q. 1.

50   Aquinas *ST*, II-II, 23,8.

51   Aquinas, *ST*, I-II, 9,1.

52   Lottin, *Morale Fondamentale*, p. 342.

53   Aquinas, *ST*, I-II, 12,2.

54   Aquinas, *De Virtutibus*, a. 12.

55   Aquinas, *De Caritate*, a. 3.

56 Dom Odon Lottin, *Au Coeur de la Morale Chrétienne* (Tournai: Desclée, 1957), p. 132.

57 Aquinas, *De Caritate*, a. 3.

58 Aquinas, *ST*, II-II, 23,8.

59 Aquinas, *III Sent.*, d. 27, q. 2.

60 Anthony J. Falanga, *Charity: The Form of the Virtues According to St. Thomas* (Washington: Catholic University of America Press, 1948), pp. 40-41.

61 Gillemann, *The Primacy of Charity*, p. 43.

62 Lottin, *Morale Fondamentale*, p. 392. Gillemann agrees that each virtue is perfected from its participation in charity, but adds that being formed from charity's love does not make every virtue charity; on the contrary, by sharing in charity's form, whatever is specific to a virtue is perfectly achieved: "In every virtue there is a special form which accounts for its particular nature, and a general form which properly makes it a virtue. These two forms cannot be extrinsic to one another, otherwise virtue would be intrinsically divided. St. Thomas adopts the expression 'forma formae' to characterize the role of charity, for charity is the higher form, and is formal in relation to the particular form of each virtue. What charity possesses by essence it communicates to the other virtues by way of participation. Charity produces in the particular virtue a 'perfection', and even more, it produces whatever perfection there is in this virtue." *The Primacy of Charity*, pp. 43-44. For an excellent historical overview on this subject of how charity can be called the form of the virtues, see Falanga, *Charity: The Form of the Virtues*, pp. 16-37.

63 Roton, *Les Habitus*, p. 106.

64 *Ibid.*, pp. 106-107.

65 Aquinas, *ST*, I-II, 61,5.

66 Robert Sokolowski, *The God of Faith and Reason* (Notre Dame: University of Notre Dame Press, 1982), p. 83.

67 Lottin, *Morale Fondamentale*, p. 167.

68 Aquinas, *De Virtutibus*, a. 13.

69   Aquinas, *ST*, I-II, 64,1.

70   Aquinas, *ST*, II-II, 23,3.

71   Aquinas, *ST*, II-II, 23,6.

72   C.A.J. Van Ouwerkerk, *Caritas et Ratio* (Nigmegen: Drukkerij Gebr Janssen, 1956), p. 88.

Chapter IV

The Gifts of the Spirit: Why They are the Perfection of the Virtues

What is remarkable about the virtues of a Christian sort is that they prepare us to rely on an agency other than our own. This is not the way we usually think of the virtues, but it is what charity works to achieve. Our argument throughout this book has been that the genius of Thomas's account of the virtues could easily be missed unless the virtues were studied as a function of charity-friendship with God. We suggested that seeing the virtues ordered by the friendship they were meant to serve would not only give us a different understanding of them, but might also challenge what we think virtue to be. Aquinas thinks differently about virtue. For him, virtue does not imply self-mastery; nor does it imply self-suffi-ciency, emphasizing so much the power of agency that eventually the virtuous person has no need of another.

That is not the way Thomas thinks of virtue, but what accounts for the difference is charity. Once we see the link between charity and the virtues our sense of virtue changes. Charity casts the virtues another way. Charity makes every virtue an expression of love, but love is a confession of need, love is an admission of our own incompleteness, and charity is a love confessing who we need is God. Anchoring the virtues in the passions may be Thomas's most brilliant methodological move because if a virtue grows from the passion of love, it works not for self-sufficiency, but surrender. Love is a passion that perfects us, and charity is a passion for God. Virtues formed in charity are borne from a longing to be transfig-ured by a love in whose likeness our happiness shines. Virtues formed in charity testify that our perfection is not something we can give ourselves, but is something we receive when we avail ourselves to the purifying love and goodness of God, a love and goodness capable of making us more than we already are; indeed, capable of giving us the radical perfection of likeness to God.

That is why we said through charity each virtue is an act of openness, an act by which God is able to determine us more deeply and completely. That is why we said the strange thing about virtues formed from charity is that the stronger we grow in them, the more defenseless we are before God. Charity gives us another kind of virtue. The strategy of virtues formed in charity is not to increase self-determination, but to provide the openness and freedom God needs to enter our life and re-make us from within. Charity reverses how we usually think about the virtues because the power of charity-formed virtues-their explicit activity-is receptivity to the love by which we are healed. As Thomas says, if God is our good, virtue which unites us with God "cannot be caused through human acts originating in reason, but is produced in us by the divine operation alone. And so Augustine's definition of this virtue includes the words, 'which God works in us without us.' "[1]

Once we acknowledge the special function of charity's virtues, we can better understand why Thomas sees their perfection in the Gifts of the Spirit. It is a consequence of love. The purpose of any love is to open us to and form us in the good of what we love. As an appetite, love is the continual, passionate activity of being related to the object of our love so that what we love ultimately possesses us. Such is the secret of love, such is the splendor of charity. Love is the recognition that we are perfected not by ourselves, but by what we love. This is why the charity-formed virtues give birth to the Gifts. Love strains for total openness, absolute receptivity to what is loved, and charity abides as an invitation to God to come to us in the Spirit and make us whole.

The connection Thomas makes between charity and the Gifts suggests that our most perfect activity is receptivity to the Trinity of Friendship, the Spirit of Love. As Ilien notes, for Thomas, "Caritas ...est...participatio quaedam infinitae caritatis quae est Spiritus

Sanctus,"[2] and the fullness of such participation in the lovelife of God is exactly what the Gifts of the Spirit represent. Charity is beatitude because our most perfect activity is a participation in God. The Spirit is the fullness of charity because the most sublime possibility of this love is a friendship which renders us so intimate to God that our life is no longer something apart from God, but a full sharing in and conforming to the goodness of God; in short, the fullness of charity is to live in the Spirit.

The argument of this book has been that the primacy Thomas gives charity in his moral theology reveals an interconnectedness between the passions and the virtues, as well as the virtues and the Gifts. In chapter two we established the primacy of love in Thomistic ethics and showed how this gave a different sense to the virtues. Chapter three focused this argument by examining what happened to virtues formed from charity's love. This chapter will complete our argument by suggesting why it is to be expected that virtues whose purpose is to make us friends with God would reach their perfection in the Gifts. The Gifts of the Spirit are in no way an afterthought to Aquinas's account of the virtues, but are entailed by charity-friendship with God. Thomas concludes his moral theology with the Gifts because the intention of the charity-formed virtues is to hand us over to God. That charity's virtues blossom forth in the Gifts-that friends of God are led by the Spirit-is hardly fortuitous; indeed, a friendship with God that does not break forth in the Spirit witnesses a love that has not reached its fullness through virtue and grace. The Gifts of the Spirit are not superfluous to the virtues, but exactly the kinds of activities for which charity prepares. The strategy of charity, as well as its wisdom, is to be the kind of activity which makes us supple to the Spirit of Life. For as Thomas says,

> Thus it is written: 'They that are led by the Spirit of God are sons of God and heirs;' and 'Your good Spirit will lead me into a right land.' For no one can attain the inheritance of that land of the blessed unless he is moved and led by the Holy Spirit. Hence, to attain the end, it is necessary for a man to have the Gifts of the Holy Spirit.[3]

A. Why the Gifts are Needed

The best way to understand what the Gifts of the Spirit are and how they are distinguished from the virtues is first to examine why they are necessary. The rationale for the Gifts of the Spirit parallels Aquinas's argument for the necessity of grace and the infused virtues: in order to act towards an end, an agent has to be proportionate to the end. A conformity between an agent and the end she or he is called to attain is demanded. Otherwise, Thomas reasons, there is no way the end can be achieved. Since the supernatural goodness of God is an end which surpasses our natural capacities, there must be infused, along with grace, the theological and supernatural moral virtues.[4]

But is supernatural virtue sufficient for a supernatural end? In his study of the Gifts, Stanislas J. Kolipinski says no. Though supernatural, the theological and infused moral virtues can never wholly achieve the end for which they are intended because no matter how deep the love which informs them, they remain our acts, human acts, and not God's. No act, Kolipinski says, which proceeds from human agency is capable of a supernatural end because our acts, no matter how good, cannot conform adequately to the goodness of God. The problem is the inherent limitation of human agency. To possess an end a person has to be conformed to it; however, where the end is the supernatural goodness of God, human agency falls short. Acts which proceed from human agency will always fall short of a supernatural end because no matter how deeply and richly we love God, we cannot, by virtue of our own activities, gain God.

That is why union with God is ultimately not a matter of our own achievements, but of redemption, the work of a love alone which is capable of perfect conformity to God. The only love capable of God is God's love. Put differently, only God has the agency requisite for attaining God; consequently, we attain God not principally through our own activities, but through a love which allows God to do for us what we cannot do for ourselves. We are saved when we let ourselves be befriended. Kolipinski says there is no better word than 'gift' to describe what accounts for salvation. It is not our achievement, but a gift, not a reward owed us, but a blessing. That Thomas sees the virtues perfected in the Gifts, our agency perfected in God's, reminds us that redemption is not a measure of our own goodness, but God's.[5]

If we consider the goal of our life is God, how can we possess God? This is the question which best explains why the Gifts are necessary for the perfect assimilation of our life unto God, and how the Gifts are distinguished from the virtues. It is a matter of agency. An act is completely good only when it accomplishes or conforms to the goodness of its end. A Christian's end is God, and God is the measure of a virtue's goodness because only acts which conform to the goodness of God are capable of God. But the rule or measure by which an act's goodness is determined also indicates the kind of agency necessary for such goodness to be achieved,[6] and that is why all our actions fall short of supernatural happiness with God. The only acts capable of securing for us perfect likeness to God are not our acts but God's. Only God has the agency, the quality of goodness, capable of a love that can make us like God. As Edward O'Connor says, there are certain defects "intrinsic to virtue," certain defects endemic to human activity, which are only removed by a superior agency.[7] Or, as Silvan Rouse says,

> We cannot act perfectly and of ourselves as sons of God through them [the theological virtues]. For while these virtues are supernatural in their very substance and have a Divine Regulation, they are infused into and conditioned by human faculties....Hence it is necessary that God Himself direct the soul to its final end.[8]

That only the Gifts can complete the work of virtue follows the interpretation of the virtues we have been proposing. Linking the virtues to the passions and making each virtue an expression of love indicated that our perfection is not something we accomplish, but something we receive. Our perfection lies on the other side of virtue in the good where our wholeness is found, and that means the virtues are perfecting only insofar as they are activities of openness, only insofar as they render us receptive to a love we must suffer if we are to be good. In this sense, the virtues intend the Gifts. As gestures of love, they stand as invitations to another love to bring our own love to completion. The Gifts are the hope of the virtues because every virtue formed from charity acknowledges a need for another love to complete it. The charity-formed virtues are a plea to God to do for us what we cannot do for ourselves. Charity makes every virtue a homage to a love it needs but can never proffer of its own. Charity makes every virtue a confession of helplessness, a confession of absolute, inescapable need, because we cannot love God enough to be made like God; we can only love God enough to receive God, to be open to God, to suffer the love which makes us like God. The charity-formed virtues intend the Gifts because only the love of God can bring our own love to rest. Our happiness is an activity of love which exceeds us, a love which surpasses our utmost ability to resemble it. Virtue is exhausted at the limit of our own agency, and it is at that point that our love calls out to another love to sate the desire from which it began. In other words, virtue's real strength is its capacity to hand us over to a love which surpasses us.

And that love is a Gift. The Spirit of Love is not something wholly different from charity, but what happens to charity at the limit of virtue. At some point in the Christian moral life our love is exhausted by the very desire which fires it; but that charity's love gives birth to the Spirit signals that virtue dies not in emptiness, but in God. That charity is a love which ultimately breaks forth in the Spirit testifies not that we love God in vain, but that our love is most perfect when it is the Spirit, when we can no longer resist the friendship, the happiness, and the life God eternally wants to give. As we emphasized in chapter one, charity is based on a communication of God's happiness. That is the clue to understanding what charity makes of us. Charity is God's desire to share the friendship life of God with us completely. Charity is God's desire to dwell in us, to make God's life our own, but such happiness is possible only when our love has made God's love irresistible. The virtue of charity works not to make us self-sufficient, but dependent on God. The virtue of charity works not to make us self-possessed, but joyfully receptive to a love which grants us the only happiness in which genuine peace is found. As we said in chapter one, the Spirit is not charity in the sense that we are only passive instruments of God's love and not the agents of our own actions; but the Spirit is the love charity seeks for it is when we are possessed by God that we are most friends of God, and, therefore, happiest.

B. What the Gifts are and How They are Related to the Virtues

It is important to recognize that the Gifts are related to the virtues not as something independent of the virtues or extrinsic to the virtues, but as the shape virtues born from charity finally take. Like the virtues, the Gifts are a function of the charity-friendship we have with God because they describe how agency is expressed in the person in whom charity is perfected. The Gifts do not replace the virtues; rather, they represent how the virtues of one whose lifetime has been a friendship with God are most perfectly expressed. The definitive formation of the virtues by charity are the Gifts of the Spirit, for that is how the agency of one who has habitually been a friend of God is finally qualified.

The Gifts do not appear as something extraneous to the virtues; the Gifts are the final and most perfect development of virtue rendered through charity. As we said in chapter three, the form a virtue takes and the goodness it achieves is relative to the friendship one has with God. The Gifts of the Spirit are not autonomous to the virtues, but virtue's most splendid possibility, virtue's highest achievement of goodness, because they are the activities of one whose friendship with God is so complete that God has become the principle of all his or her activities. The Gifts are the most excellent activities of the charity-formed virtues because the Spirit is the ultimate effect friendship love has on agency. The Gifts of the Spirit emerge from and are the perfection of the virtues of a friend of God because action is always relative to agency, and the Gifts are the actions of the person whose will is so much one with God's that it is the Spirit.

The Gifts are possible only where charity has long been at work. The Gifts not only presuppose the theological virtues, principally charity, but are also derived from them because, as Thomas explains, the Spirit can only move the person who is already united with God:

> The soul of man is not moved by the Holy Spirit unless it is somehow united with him, just as a tool is not moved by the craftsman except through contact or some other union. But man's primary union with God comes through faith, hope and charity. Hence, the virtues are presupposed by the Gifts, as a sort of root from which the Gifts spring. Hence all the Gifts pertain to these three virtues as derivations from them.[9]

Similarly, Lottin says the Gifts are the "fruits" of charity[10] harvested from the theological virtues[11] because they represent the ultimate effect those virtues have on agency. Pepin, too, emphasizes that "on ne doit pas regarder les dons du Saint-Esprit comme independants des vertus theologales, dont ils sont, pour ainsi dire, la ramification et l'epanouissement."[12]

The key to understanding the Gifts is to ask, "What does love do to us?" As we said in chapter two, love is a movement which begins not in itself, but in the thing loved. To love is to be moved by what we love. The Gifts of the Spirit are the perfection of a passion for God, indeed the only way that passion can be satisfied, because to have the Gifts is not only to be moved by what we love, but also to be possessed by it, to be moved from within, God's love working in and through our own. With the Gifts of the Spirit, God's love is no longer something to which we tend, but is the innermost principle of all we do. All love is a response to what is loved, and the fullness of charity is a responsiveness to God so far-reaching that everything we do is a movement of the one we love.

That is the kind of radical penetration of the self a passion for God achieves. To love anything is to acquire its form and to be remade in its likeness. To love God is to be ruled by the Spirit because the Spirit, that Trinity of friendship, is the form of God's love, and that is the form charity brings to all our behavior. The Gifts are a function of the agency made possible through friendship for God. They mark the deeds of the person who has fallen com-

pletely, finally, and unconditionally in love with God. As Lottin
says so well, the Gifts are entailed by charity because the aim of
friendship is to be disposed perfectly to the desires of the friend.
The Gifts are the most complete realization of friendship love and
its ultimate satisfaction. They describe a person who is so disposed
to God and so docile before God that God's will is the power by
which she acts. As Lottin writes,

> Quand on aime une personne, on s'attache à ne rien lui refuser, à realiser son
> bon plaisir en toutes choses; la volonté se fait docile à toutes les manifesta-
> tions de ce bon plaisir et elle vit en perpétuelle disponibilité à l'égard des
> désirs de la personne aimée. Cette loi qui régit l'amour humain règle aussi
> nos rapports avec Dieu: la charité crée une souplesse d'âme qui rend la
> volonté parfaitement docile aux inspirations du Saint-Esprit.[13]

The relationship we have sketched between charity and the Gifts
enables us to mark clearly how the Gifts are both alike and different from the virtues. It is notable that the Gifts are derived from
the virtues, for that means the Gifts, though more excellent than
the virtues, are, nonethless, a form of virtue. The Gifts, Froget explains, are virtues insofar as they "are habits or dispositions towards
good, which exist in the soul as determined and continuous qualities."[14] They are not passing or superfluous activities, unexpected
signs of the presence of God, but habitual ways of behavior which
portray a quality intrinsic to the person. The Gifts are what we ex-
pect the behavior of God's best friends to be. They are habits. The
Gifts are how a life of friendship with God has disposed one to act.
Like the virtues, they are patterned ways of acting for the sake of a
certain end. Like the virtues, they are perfecting because they
render both an action and its agent good. The Gifts, like the
virtues, dispose us to our most excellent activities. Thus, as Thomas
suggests, the Gifts are a kind of virtue inasmuch as they incline the
agent to right action. Too, they share virtue's end, namely union
with God. The Gifts and the virtues are not opposed, nor are they
entirely distinct; rather, the Gifts are virtues, but what distinguishes
them from the virtues is the agency from which they proceed.
Thomas writes:

So far as the meaning of the words is concerned, there is no opposition between gift and virtue. For the meaning of the term virtue comes from the fact
that virtue perfects man so that he may act rightly, as was said above, whereas
the meaning of the term gift comes from the relationship of that which is
given to the cause from which it derives. But there is no reason why that
which comes from another as a gift should not perfect a person for right action; especially since we said above that certain virtues are infused into us by
God. Hence, on this basis, a Gift cannot be distinguished from a virtue.[15]

It is this difference in agency which accounts for the superior excellence of the Gifts. The Gifts do possess an excellence the virtues
lack. There is a consummate goodness proper to the Gifts that the
charity-formed virtues can never achieve because the Gifts are activities of God. As Thomas says, "These Gifts are sometimes called
virtues in the common meaning of the word virtue. However, there
is something in them that transcends the common meaning of
virtue, in that they are divine virtues and perfect man in so far as he
is moved by God."[16] The Gifts are God's virtues. The Gifts are
how God is virtuous, how God is good, how God is perfect love.
They are, as Bernard describes, something of the "last word" of
virtue, virtue's highest possible excellence, those activities which
are unsurpassed in rendering both deeds and their possessor good,
because the Gifts are good as God is good.[17] The Gifts are the
virtues of one absolutely possessed by God.

That is what has to be remembered about the Gifts. They are
God acting not outside us but from within. The Gifts are more perfect than the virtues because we are the agents of virtue but God is
the agent of Gift; however, with the Gifts God's agency has
become our own. What accounts for the Gifts is a determination of
agency effected through love. The Gifts signal a transformation of
agency so complete that it is in virtue of God that the friend of
God acts. "The Gifts surpass the common perfection of the virtues,
not as regards the kinds of works done," Thomas explains, "but as
regards the mode of operation, inasmuch as man is moved in the
case of the Gifts by a higher principle."[18] With the Gifts, men and
women are moved by God.[19]   Thomas says the Gifts are
"perfections which dispose a man to follow the prompting of the
Holy Spirit well,"[20] and as Silvan Rouse comments, this means the

soul "is moved by the Spirit without moving itself. This motion depends totally on the Spirit, it precedes human deliberation. God alone is moving and the operation is attributed to Him."[21] Bernard, too, stresses that the Gifts are habits, a perfection of virtue, for they signify that there is in one an "habitual disposition" to be docile to the promptings of God.[22]

The Gifts are the virtues of one in whom God lives unhindered. They are a consequence of charity and an expression of charity because it is only a deep and abiding love for God that makes possible permanent openness to God. The Gifts are the virtues of the man or woman made one with God in love. They are an expression of friendship; in fact, they are friendship's delight because the Gifts represent union with the God who is our happiness. Made one with us through friendship, God's Spirit of Love dwells in the soul not provisionally, but permanently,[23] "inaugurating here below that life of union and beatitude," that perfect friendship, "which is to be consummated in heaven."[24]   As Silvan Rouse explains, the Gifts are the perfection of charity for they signal a union with God so complete that God is more intimate to us than we are to ourself. With the Gifts, it is by the 'other self' of God that we are:

> The Holy Spirit not only comes to the soul and abides in it; He not only endows it with his multiple gifts, but He also acts in the human soul and moves it toward its final end. Made one spirit with Him, we are moved more intimately by Him than by reason. The motion of the Spirit is exercised in the depths of man's heart. It affects his integral spiritual activity, both intellectual and affective. It is a motion which is proper to God alone; only He can directly move the spiritual faculties of man. It is a work of interiority which corresponds to the innerness of the Divine Agent.[25]

To act in virtue of God and not ourselves, to be moved by divine agency instead of our own, did not signify a loss of freedom for Thomas, but freedom's highest possibility, freedom's perfection, because to be absorbed wholly in God was what charity always desired. The Gifts of the Spirit are not inflicted upon the friend of God against her will, but express a harmony of wills which is every friendship's purpose to achieve. To be moved by the Spirit is to will what God wills as God wills, and for the friend of God such docility is joy. In response to the objection that with the Gifts men and women seem to be acted upon by God against their will, Thomas says,

> This reasoning is based on the case of an instrument which does not act but is only acted upon. Man, however, is not that sort of instrument; but he is moved by the Holy Spirit in such a way that he also acts, in so far as he has free will.[26]

This is why Lithard's insight that the virtues are "operative" habits and the Gifts "receptive" habits is so apt.[27] They are both virtues, but the Gifts are virtues of a higher form because we are most perfected not when we act, but when we are acted upon by the perfect goodness of God. As Aquinas's definition of virtue makes clear, an act's excellence is proportionate to its capacity to achieve its end. Our most excellent activity is not our own, but God's. Virtue's perfect form in us is not activity but receptivity, because the divine end is fully attained only through the divine love. God is a happiness ultimately reached not through our own love, but God's. God is a goodness we enjoy not because we master it, but only because through charity we have become open enough to receive it exactly as it is, a Gift. The paradox of Aquinas's account of the virtues is unflinching: our greatest moral possibility is not to act, but to let ourselves be acted upon by God, for it is when we suffer the divine love that we become most like it. What Silvan Rouse says about the Gift of Understanding is equally true for all the Gifts of the Spirit.

> The perfection of this operative habit of donal Understanding is to receive, without resistance, all the motion which the Spirit of Understanding communicates and to allow it to pass, unaltered, to the work which the Principle Agent intends. For the pneumatic Christian this is the eminent form of activity-acting freely from a suffering of divine realities under the active direction of the Holy Spirit.[28]

Or, as Victor Lithard comments, the moral life for Aquinas has two phases, the ascetical and the mystical.[29] In the ascetical phase, we are the primary agents and our love for God is the principle of our activity; however, in the mystical phase God is the agent of our activity and God's love is the principle of our behavior. In the mystical phase of the moral life, the center of agency shifts. Charity commences in the ascetical phase of the moral life but works toward the mystical phase because then the love of God operates freely in our lives, purifying us, changing us, transforming us in a likeness to God before which our own love can only pale. The mystical life is the perfection of the moral life because a friendship love which counts God's good as its own is only satisfied when it is ruled by what it foremost desires. Bernard comments,

> La vie mystique sort d'un fond qui est, dès l'abord, beaucoup plus passif qu'actif, et tend à le devenir de plus en plus. C'est même en cela que consiste l'élément fondamental de l'état mystique, comme l'a très bien montré le P. Joret. L'âme n'a plus alors d'autre activité que d'adhérer. Toute sa perfection est d'avoir la souplesse d'un membre pour se laisser mouvoir, ou la délicatesse d'un instrument à se laisser toucher. Il n'est point de meilleure coopération pour elle que celle d'un complet abandon. Il n'importe plus tant d'agir que d' "être agi", non plus tant de se posséder soi-même que de se laisser dépossedér de soi pour être mieux posséde de Dieu.[30]

C. Why Moral Wisdom is the Harvest of Love

Being ruled by the goodness of God is the highest goodness of which we are capable. Intimacy is a matter of likeness and similarity of character, a kinship acquired through devotion to the same good, and that every virtue is perfected in a Gift indicates that we become good not solely of ourselves, but more properly as we have shared in and acquired the goodness of God. Discerning the good is a virtue Thomas calls prudence, an uncanny ability to recognize the good and see how the good can and needs to be done; however, even though prudence is an intellectual virtue, it is an ability born not only from reflection but also from love. There is no such thing as goodness apart from God, and that is why we rightly learn the good through friendship with God. The validity of our moral perceptions is contingent upon the depth of friendship we enjoy with God. That is why prudence depends on charity and reaches its perfection in the Gift of Counsel.[31]

We only see the good clearly and know how goodness is to be done when we have acquired the form of goodness itself. We have to have charity to know and do the good because moral wisdom is not so much a matter of study but of kinship, not so much a matter of reason but of love. Noble is right that we are truly prudent only when God counsels all our activity,[32] because knowledge of the good is a matter of union with the Good, and there is no more penetrating knowledge of the good than that which comes when we are moved in all things by God. "We have said that the wisdom under discussion," Thomas writes, "implies a certain rightness of judgment in contemplating and in consulting divine things. Now regarding both acts, the degree of wisdom will vary according to the degree of union with divine things."[33]

Aristotle was right when he said friendship was necessary for us to be good. What Aquinas adds is that if we want to be good, friendship with God must be the principle activity of our life. We can only know the good when we are good. We become good by acquiring the form of goodness, and that, as we have seen, is possible only through charity's love. This is why Thomas says "wisdom presupposes charity."[34]   This is why Mouroux says, "In human, moral, and spiritual matters, it is necessary to love to be able to know, and it is necessary to love well to be able to know well."[35] And this is why Lavaud says we rightly know the good only through a "sort of interior experience" we have with God.[36]

Moral wisdom does not precede love but is the harvest of love. We noted in chapter one that Thomas emphasizes consent over choice. Doing good balances not so much on freedom as discernment. To discern is to see clearly, but, as Gilson explains, for Thomas we must see the good "from within rather than from without, to be impregnated with it, to absorb it into one's very substance,"[37] and this suggests goodness is known not so much intellectually but affectionately. Goodness is more a matter of consent than choice because goodness is much more something we suffer from love than create through freedom. Thomas explains,

A correct judgment made through rational investigation belongs to the wisdom which is an intellectual virtue. But to judge aright through a certain fellowship with them belongs to that wisdom which is the gift of the Holy Spirit. Dionysius says that Hierotheus is perfected in divine things for 'he not only learns about them but suffers them as well.' Now this sympathy, or connaturality with divine things, results from charity which unites us to God.[38]

D. Conclusion

Thomas ends his treatise on the Gifts with a discussion of the Fruits of the Spirit, qualities which accrue to the one whose union with God is complete. The Fruits of the Spirit are love, joy, and peace:

> The love of charity is necessarily followed by joy. For the lover rejoices in being united with the one he loves....The perfection of joy, however, is peace.... For one cannot have perfect joy in the good which he loves if he is disturbed by other things. Likewise, he whose heart is perfectly satisfied by one thing, is not able to be disturbed by anything else, since he values everything else as nothing; thus it is written, 'Great peace have those who love your name, and there is nothing to make them stumble.[39]

The Fruits of the Spirit bring a quieting of desire. They come to the person whose passion for God has been met. It is fitting that Thomas ends his moral theology with a love satisfied and a desire fulfilled because that was the aim with which he began. For Thomas, morality is passion, a love thirsting for the good which is our happiness, and the *Prima Secundae* stands as Thomas's conviction that our happiness has to be God. The only way we find joy and peace is if we love the right things in the right way. The moral theology of the *Prima Secundae* is Thomas's plea for us to love God with whole heart and soul, for God alone can bring peace and healing to our hearts.

The argument of this book has been that charity is the key to interpreting Thomas's account of the passions, the virtues, and the Gifts of the Spirit. Charity is our happiness because happiness is an active participation in the God whose goodness is our perfection. The goal of the moral life for Thomas is to get us to God, but, as we have seen, going to God is not so much a matter of change of place, but change of person. God is an end we attain not by moving towards it, but by becoming like it, and likeness is always a work of love. We are happiest when we become as much like God as possible, and charity is necessary for that because there is no greater likeness to God than that which friendship renders. Likeness is the work of charity because through friendship love we are formed in the goodness of God.

Reading the *Prima Secundae* from the perspective of charity shows us that for Aquinas morality begins in the passions and must be a passion for God. It shows us that every virtue is a work of love and true virtue is formed from charity's love. That makes every virtue an expression of need, an act of openness and vulnerability to a God who offers us a fullness we could never attain on our own. The Gifts are the perfection of virtue because virtue is a perfecting activity, and charity knows ultimately we are perfected by a love we can never equal, but only receive. Thomas concludes,

> Beatitude is the last end of human life....However, ...in the case of that end which is beatitude, one moves towards it and draws near to it through the activity of the virtues, and more especially through the activity of the Gifts, if we are speaking of eternal beatitude. For in the latter case, reason does not suffice, but the Holy Spirit brings one to the end, and the Gifts perfect us for obeying and following him.[40]

Read the moral theology of the *Prima Secundae* from the rubric of charity, study the passions, the virtues, and the Gifts in its light, and this is what you learn: in those who know God best, the stalwart friends of God we call saints, love always takes the form of gratitude, for the friendship with God that is our happiness, in both its beginning and its perfection, is always but a response to a gift, a never-ending homage to a God who loves us first.

Notes

1 Aquinas, *ST*, I-II, 63,2.

2 Ilien, *Wesen*, p. 204.

3 Aquinas, *ST*, I-II, 68,2.

4 Aquinas, *ST*, I-II, 63,3.

5 Stanislas J. Kolipinski, *Le Don de L'Esprit* (Fribourg: Bureaux Des Studia Friburgensia, 1924), pp. 80-81.

6 Dom Odon Lottin, *Psychologie Et Morale Aux XII et XIII Siècles* (Louvain: Abbaye du Mont César, 1949), III, 429.

7 Edward O'Connor, "The Evolution of St. Thomas's Thought on the Gifts," *Summa Theologica* (New York: McGraw-Hill, 1973), Appendix 4, XXIV, 110-111.

8 Silvan Rouse, *The Gift of Understanding According to St. Thomas Aquinas and his Predecessors* (Rome: The Pontifical University, 1964), pp. 165-166.

9 Aquinas, *ST*, I-II, 68,4.

10 Lottin, *Morale Fondamentale*, p. 431.

11 Lottin, *Au Coeur*, p. 143.

12 Pépin, *La Charité*, pp. 165-166.

13 Lottin, *La Coeur*, pp. 128-129.

14 Barthelemy Froget, *The Indwelling of the Holy Spirit in the Souls of the Just* (Westminster, Maryland: The Newman Press, 1952), pp. 203-204.

15 Aquinas, *ST*, I-II, 68,1.

16 Aquinas, *ST*, I-II, 68,1.

17 R. Bernard, "La Vertu Infuse et Le Don Du Saint-Esprit," *La Vie Spirituelle*, XLII (1935), Suppl. 67.

18 Aquinas, *ST*, I-II, 68,2.

19 Kolipinski, *Le Don*, p. 51.

20 Aquinas, *ST*, I-II, 68,3.

21 Rouse, *The Gift*, pp. 181-182.

22 Bernard, "La Vertu Infuse," p. 71.

23 Rouse, *The Gift*, p. 188.

24 Froget, *The Indwelling*, p. 237.

25 Rouse, *The Gift*, p. 180.

26 Aquinas, *ST*, I-II, 68,3.

27 Victor Lithard, "Les Dons Du Saint-Esprit et Les Graces De La Vie Mystique," *Revue d'Ascetique et de Mystique*, XVII (1936), 170.

28 Rouse, *The Gift*, p. 193.

29 Victor Lithard, "Les Dons Du Saint-Esprit," *Revue Apologetique*, LXV (1937), 14-15.

30 Bernard, "La Vertu Infuse," p. 85.

31 Aquinas, *ST*, II-II, 52,2.

32 Henri Noble, *La Conscience Morale* (Paris: P. Lethielleux, 1923), pp. 156-157.

33 Aquinas, *ST*, II-II, 45,5.

34 Aquinas, *ST*, II-II, 45,4.

35 Mouroux, *The Christian Experience*, p. 248.

36 Leopold Lavaud, "Saint Thomas: Notes Distinctives de sa Sainteté," *Saint Thomas d'Aquin: Sa Sainteté, Sa Doctrine Spirituelle*, p. 13.

37 Gilson, *The Christian Philosophy*, p. 349.

38 Aquinas, *ST*, II-II, 45,2.

39 Aquinas, *ST*, I-II, 70,3.

40 Aquinas, *ST*, I-II, 69,1.

Bibliography

Primary Sources

Aquinas, St. Thomas. *Compendium of Theology*. Translated by Cyril Vollert. Saint Louis: B. Herder Book Co., 1947.

_____. *De Caritate*. Translated by Lottie H. Kendzierski. Milwaukee: Marquette University Press, 1960.

_____. *De Virtutibus*. Translated by John Patrick Reid, O.P. Providence: The Providence College Press, 1951.

_____. *Scriptum Super Sententiis Magistri Petri Lombardi*. 4 vols. Paris: P. Lethielleux, 1933. Vol. III.

_____. *Summa Contra Gentiles*. Translated by Vernon J. Bourke and Charles J. O'Neil. 4 vols. Garden City: Hanover House, 1956. Vols. III-IV.

_____. *Summa Theologiae*. Blackfriar's Edition. 60 vols. New York: McGraw-Hill Book Co., 1963-1974.

_____. *The Commandments of God*. Translated by Laurence Shapcote, O.P. London: Burns, Oates and Washbourne, Ltd., 1937.

Aristotle. *Nichomachean Ethics*. Translated by Martin Ostwald. Indianapolis: Bobbs-Merrill Educational Publishing Co., 1962.

Secondary Sources

A. Books

Baker, Richard. *The Thomistic Theory of the Passions and Their Influence Upon the Will*. Ann Arbor: Edwards Brothers, Inc., 1941.

Buckley, Joseph. *Man's Last End*. Saint Louis: B. Herder Book, Co., 1949.

Bullet, Gabriel. *Vertus Morales Infuses et Vertus Morales Acquises Selon St. Thomas D'Aquin*. Fribourg: Éditions Universitaires, 1958.

Cauchy, Venant. *Désir Naturel et Béatitude Chez St. Thomas*. Montreal: Fides, 1958.

Chenu, M.D. *Toward Understanding St. Thomas*. Translated by Albert M. Landry and Dominic Hughes. Chicago: Henry Regnery Co., 1964.

Egenter, Richard. *Gottesfreundschaft: Die Lehre von der Gottesfreundschaft in der Scholastik und Mystik des 12 und 13 Jahrhunderts*. Augsburg: Dr. Benno Filser, 1928.

Falanga, Anthony J. *Charity: The Form of the Virtues According to St. Thomas*. Washington: Catholic University of America Press, 1948.

Froget, Barthelemy. *The Indwelling of the Holy Spirit in the Souls of the Just*. Westminster, Maryland: The Newman Press, 1952.

Gagnon, Edouard. *Les Vertus Théologales*. Montreal: Éditions de L'Institut Pie-XI, 1960.

Geiger, Louis B. *Le Problème de L'Amour Chez Saint Thomas D'Aquin*. Montreal: Institute D'Études Médievales, 1952.

Gillemann, Gerard. *The Primacy of Charity in Moral Theology*. Translated by William F. Ryan and Andre Vachon. Westminster, Maryland: The Newman Press, 1959.

Gilson, Etienne. *Moral Values and the Moral Life*. Translated by Leo Richard Ward, C.S.C. Saint Louis: B. Herder Book Co., 1941.

_____. *The Christian Philosophy of St. Thomas Aquinas*. Translated by L.K. Shook. New York: Random House, 1956.

Guindon, Roger. *Béatitude et Théologie Morale Chez St. Thomas D'Aquin*. Ottawa: Éditions de l'Université d'Ottawa, 1956.

Hauerwas, Stanley. *Character and the Christian Life: A Study in Theological Ethics*. San Antonio: Trinity University Press, 1975.

Heris, Ch. V. *Perfection et Charité*. Paris: Éditions Alsatia, 1961.

_____. *Spirituality of Love*. Translated by David Martin. Saint Louis: B. Herder Book Co., 1965.

Horvath, Tibor. *Caritas Est in Ratione*. Münster: Aschendorff, 1966.

Ilien, Albert. *Wesen und Funktion der Liebe bei Thomas von Aquin*. Freiburg: Herder, 1975.

Johann, Robert. *The Meaning of Love*. Glen Rock, New Jersey: The Paulist Press, 1966.

Kolipinski, Stanislas J. *Le Don de L'Esprit Saint*. Fribourg: Bureaux Des Studia Friburgensia, 1924.

Leclercq, Jacques. *La Philosophie Morale de Saint Thomas Devant La Pensée Contemporaine*. Louvain: Publications Universitaires de Louvain, 1955.

_____. *Les Grandes Lignes de la Philosophie Morale*. Louvain: Publications Universitaires de Louvain, 1954.

Lottin, Dom Odon. *Au Coeur de la Morale Chrétienne*. Tournai: Desclée, 1957.

_____. *Aux Sources De Notre Grandeur Morale*. Louvain: Éditions de L'Abbaye du Mont César, 1946.

_____. *Études de Morale Histoire et Doctrine*. Gembloux: J. Duclot, 1961.

_____. *Morale Fondamentale*. Tournai: Desclée and Cie, 1954.

_____. *Psychologie et Morale Aux XII et XIII Siècles*. 6 vols. Louvain: Abbaye du Mont César, 1949-1954.

MacIntyre, Alasdair. *After Virtue*. Notre Dame, Indiana: University of Notre Dame Press, 1981.

Mouroux, Jean. *The Christian Experience*. Translated by George Lamb. New York: Sheed and Ward, 1954.

Noble, Henri. *L'Amitié Avec Dieu*. Paris: Desclée and Cie, 1932.

_____. *La Conscience Morale*. Paris: P. Lethielleux, 1923.

_____. *Les Passions Dans La Vie Morale*. 2 vols. Paris: P. Lethielleux, 1931-1932.

O'Connor, William R. *The Eternal Quest*. New York: Longman, Green and Co., 1947.

Pépin, R.P. Adrien. *La Charité Envers Dieu*. Paris: Nouvelles Éditions Latines, 1952.

Philippe, Paul. *Le Rôle de L'Amitié Dans La Vie Chrétienne Selon Saint Thomas D'Aquin*. Rome: Angelicum, 1938.

Pinckaers, Servais. *Le Renouveau de la Morale*. Castermann, 1964.

Rohmer, Jean. *La Finalité Morale Chez Les Théologiens de Saint Augustin à Duns Scot*. Paris: Libraire Philosophique J. Vrin, 1939.

Roton, Placide de. *Les Habitus: Leur Caractère Spirituel*. Paris: Labergerie, 1934.

Rouse, Silvan. *The Gift of Understanding According to St. Thomas Aquinas and his Predecessors*. Rome: The Pontifical University, 1964.

Rousselot, P. *Pour L'Histoire du Problème de L'Amour au Moyen Âge*. Paris, 1933.

Sertillanges, A.D. *La Philosophie Morale de Saint Thomas D'Aquin*. Paris: Librairie Félix Alcan, 1922.

Sokolowski, Robert. *The God of Faith and Reason*. Notre Dame, Indiana: University of Notre Dame Press, 1982.

Thils, G. *Tendances Actuelles en Théologie Morale*. Gembloux: J. Duclot, 1940.

Van Ouwerkerk, C.A.J. *Caritas et Ratio*. Nigmegen: Janssen, 1956.

Van Roey, J.E. *De Virtute Charitatis*. Mechliniae: H. Dessain, 1929.

Vann, Gerald. *St. Thomas Aquinas*. New York: Benziger Brothers, 1947.

Weisheipl, James A. *Friar Thomas D'Aquino: His Life, Thought, and Work*. Garden City: Doubleday and Co., 1974.

B. Articles

Bernard, R. "La Vertu Infuse et Le Don du Saint-Esprit," *La Vie Spirituelle*, XLII (1935), Suppl. 65-90.

Broglie, Guy de. "Charité: Essai d'une Synthèse Doctrinale," *Dictionnaire de Spiritualité*, II (1953), col. 661-691.

Carpentier, R. "Vers une Morale de La Charité," *Gregorianum*, XXXIV (1953), 32-55.

Coconnier, M. "Ce Qu'est La Charité d'Après Saint Thomas d'Aquin," *Revue Thomiste*, XIV (1906), 5-30.

Cooper, John M. "Aristotle on Friendship," *Essays on Aristotle's Ethics*, ed. Amelie O. Rorty. Berkeley: University of California Press, 1980, 301-340.

Deman, Thomas. "Eudémonisme et Charité en Théologie Morale," *Ephemerides Theologicae Lovanienses*, XXIX (1953), 41-57.

DeVooght, P. "Y A-T-Il des Vertus Morales Infuses?" *Ephemerides Theologicae Lovanienses*, X (1933), 232-242.

Keller, Joseph. "De Virtute Caritatis ut Amicitia Quadam Divina," *Xenia Thomistica Theologica*, II (1925), 233-276.

Lavaud, Benoit and Keller, Joseph. "La Charité Comme Amitié d'Après S. Thomas," *Revue Thomiste*, XII (1929), 445-475.

Lavaud, Leopold. "Saint Thomas: Notes Distinctives de sa Sainteté," *Saint Thomas d'Aquin: Sa Sainteté, Sa Doctrine Spirituelle*, ed. Leopold Lavaud. Saint-Maximin: Éditions de la Vie Spirituelle, 3-20.

Lithard, Victor. "Les Dons du Saint-Esprit," *Revue Apologetique*, LXV (1937), 5-22.

_____. "Les Dons du Saint-Esprit et Les Graces de la Vie Mystique," *Revue d'Ascetique et de Mystique*, XVII (1936), 169-180.

Mersch, E. "La Grace et Les Vertus Théologales," *Nouvelle Revue Théologique*, LXIV (1937), 802-817.

Neveut, E. "La Vertu de Charité: Son Caractère Surnaturel," *Divus Thomas*, XL (1937), 145 sq.

Noble, Henri. "L'Amitié Avec Dieu," *La Vie Spirituelle*, XII (1925), 3-15.

_____. "Synthèse de La Doctrine Morale de Saint Thomas," *Saint Thomas d'Aquin: Sa Sainteté, Sa Doctrine Spirituelle*, ed. Leopold Lavaud. Saint-Maximin: Editions de la Vie Spirituelle, 55 sq.

O'Connor, Edward D. "The Evolution of St. Thomas' Thought on the Gifts," *Summa Theologiae*, New York: McGraw-Hill Book Co., Appendix 4, XXIV (1973), 110-130.

Pinckaers, Servais. "La Morale de Saint Thomas Est-elle Chrétienne?" *Nova et Vetera*, LI (1976), 93-107.

Roland-Gosselin, M.D. "Le Sermon Sur La Montagne et La Théologie Thomiste," *Revue des Sciences Philosophiques et Theologiques*, XVII (1928), 201-234.

Schultes, R.M. "De Caritate ut Forma Virtutum," *Divus Thomas*, XXXI (1928), 5-28.

Simonin, H.D. "Autour de la Solution Thomiste du Problème de L'Amour," *Archives d'Histoire Doctrinale et Littéraire du Moyen Âge*, VI (1932), 174-276.

Van Roey, J.E. "De Charitate Forma Virtutum," *Ephemerides Theologicae Louvaniensis*, I (1924), 43 sq.

Wohlman, Avital. "L'Élaboration des Éléments Aristotéliciens dans La Doctrine Thomiste de L'Amour," *Revue Thomiste*, LXXXII (1982), 247-269

DATE DUE

DEC 22 2000			